Breaking the Silence

The Church Responds to Domestic Violence

Breaking
the Silence

The Church Responds
to Domestic Violence

Anne O. Weatherholt

MOREHOUSE PUBLISHING

An imprint of Church Publishing Incorporated
Harrisburg—New York

Unless otherwise noted, the Scripture quotations contained herein are from the New Revised Standard Version Bible, copyright © 1989 by the Division of Christian Education of the National Council of Churches of Christ in the U.S.A. Used by permission. All rights reserved.

Morehouse Publishing, 4775 Linglestown Road,
Harrisburg, PA 17112

Morehouse Publishing, 445 Fifth Avenue, New York, NY 10016

Morehouse Publishing is an imprint of
Church Publishing Incorporated.

Cover design by Brenda Klinger

Interior design by Ronda Scullen

Library of Congress Cataloging-in-Publication Data

Weatherholt, Anne O.
 Breaking the silence : the church responds to domestic violence /
Anne O. Weatherholt.
   p. cm.
 Includes bibliographical references.
 ISBN 978-0-8192-2320-3 (pbk.)
 1. Family violence—Religious aspects—Christianity. 2. Church work with problem families. 3. Church work with abused women.
I. Title.
 BV4438.5.W43 2008
 261.8'327—dc22
                  2008023751

Printed in the United States of America

08 09 10 11 12 13   10 9 8 7 6 5 4 3 2 1

Contents

Acknowledgments

I wish to thank the following persons who were instrumental in helping me take a small manuscript and turn it into a useful resource:

The Rev. Wes Wubbenhorst, Youth Missioner in the Episcopal Diocese of Maryland, who found a way to draw attention to the need for this book;

Dian Nelson, my dear friend, who read the first draft, corrected many errors, gave me lots of suggestions from the local paper and World Wide Web, and helped me learn how to document my research;

To my family, Allan my husband, my boys Daniel and Stephen, who quietly and patiently went about their lives in our home while I wrote, and always showed interest and pride for what I was doing;

To the director and staff at CASA (Citizens Assisting and Sheltering the Abused) in Hagerstown, those on the "front line" who provided answers to my many technical questions about helping the victims of domestic violence;

The staff at Church Publishing who were so gracious and encouraging;

And to my colleagues in ministry who kept saying this book was greatly needed.

Introduction

Every day, women from all walks of life are intimidated, beaten, and sexually assaulted by their intimate partners. You already know someone who has felt the terror and intimidation of domestic violence. According to a 2006 Harris Poll quoted on the National Domestic Violence Hotline Statistics in June 2008, approximately 33 million or 15% of all U.S. adults admit that they were a victim of domestic violence. Furthermore, six in ten adults claim that they know someone personally who has experienced domestic violence.[1] More than three women are murdered by their husbands or boyfriends every day,[2] and one in three teens reports knowing a friend or a peer who has been hit, punched, or slapped by his or her date.[3] Abusers come from all socio-economic levels, all occupations, all ethnic and religious groups. Often, their victims are unwilling or feel unable to leave their homes or their abusive partners.

---

1.   www.ndvh.org/educate/abuse_in_america.html.

2.   Bureau of Justice Statistics Crime Data Brief, *Intimate Partner Violence, 1993–2001*, February 2003.

3.   Teenage Research Unlimited. Findings from study commissioned by Liz Claiborne Inc. to investigate the level of and attitudes towards dating abuse among American teenagers aged 13 to 18 [online] 2005 Feb [cited 2006 Mar 20]. Available at www. loveisnotabuse.com/statistics_abuseandteens.htm.

Unlike many crimes that the general public recognizes as illegal—breaking and entering, assault, robbery, rape, drunk driving—domestic violence is a crime, usually hidden, that often goes unrecognized. Even when people may suspect that abuse is taking place, they may not know how to respond, or may feel it is none of their business. Domestic violence takes place in private between two persons who are supposed to love one another. The extent of the abuse and the time period over which it occurs are often underestimated by those in the situation and by those who may have suspected that abuse is taking place. Because it happens in private, in the "sanctity" of the home, abuse is difficult to prevent, to identify, to stop, and to prosecute.

My husband and I are Episcopal priests and state police chaplains. We keep police scanners on in our home and offices, and almost every day we hear law enforcement officers called to incidents of domestic violence. Many of the calls are frightening, with sounds of yelling in the background and reports of the presence of weapons, and the situations are fraught with danger for the victims and the law enforcement officers. As we counsel these frontline officers after a critical incident, we hear their frustration with this ongoing and pernicious behavior. But we have also counseled those in abusive relationships in our churches, families for whom we have performed weddings and baptisms, and we serve on community boards for agencies that assist victims of domestic abuse. When I was first ordained, I performed a wedding for a young couple in the chapel of the college where I was serving as chaplain. About a year later, I ran into the wife in a grocery store and was stunned to find that they were divorced. She told me she was all right now, but that her husband had beat her after they were married. She told me that before they were married, he used to hit the dog. Soon thereafter, I joined a group of women meeting to begin the process for establishing a shelter for abused women in Frederick, Maryland. That shelter is there today.

The roots of domestic violence lie deep within a society that still values men more than women and teaches men to view women as inferior and sexual objects. Most of those abused are women, but men can also be abused by partners who intimidate, insult, and debase them, and men may suffer physical abuse, as well. In order to avoid awkward and cumbersome phrasing in this book, we have sometimes used the male pronoun for the abuser and the female for the one who is abused, but this is not intended to exclude or diminish the experiences of male victims. Please see the section specifically for male victims in chapter 3.

The flames of the violence are fanned by a culture that desensitizes us to feelings of revulsion and deadens our reactions by frequent exposure to violent acts that we see all around us on television, movies, and via the World Wide Web. History shows us that the faith community is also culpable in denying or supporting domestic abuse through traditional teachings that empower men and weaken women, and through an emphasis on upholding the doctrines of marriage and family while overlooking the behavior that is actually demonstrated in the home. People who are abused hesitate to turn to their church, fearing condemnation or the possibility that their minister will advise them to return home and try harder to make the marriage work. The faith that is supposed to offer hope and freedom to those in captivity is empty for those who are told that suffering is redemptive, and vows are unbreakable.

This book was written as a response to several Resolutions from the General Convention of the Episcopal Church in 1988 and 2000. Resolution 2000-C025 reads in part "that the 73rd General Convention calls upon every congregation within the church to designate at least one Sunday a year . . . for special prayers for all whose lives have been affected by any form of . . . family violence." The resolution further states that education be offered about "practical, pastoral, spiritual and/or theological issues related to the problems of . . . domestic violence," and that congregations be urged to make active and ongoing response to these problems in their local community.[4]

While most of us tend to shy away from this subject and deny its pervasive reality, learning about domestic violence and reaching out to help the victims are not sad and depressing tasks. Barbara Reed Martin, current CEO of Heartly House, Inc. in Frederick, Maryland, an emergency shelter, speaks with great hope about work with victims of domestic violence. She says, "When women ask for help, life-transforming work happens."[5]

Life-transforming work is the mission of the church, and when a faith community is educated, challenged, and involved in the issue of domestic violence, life-transforming work will happen. No single resource can provide all the answers. This book may help you get started, but the written word is only a tool to be used by compassionate people who act on their baptismal vows "to respect the dignity of every human being"[6] and reach out with their hands, their time, and their resources to lift up those who have been battered down by domestic violence.

---

4. General Convention Research Report, 2000-CO25. Available at http://www.episcopalarchives.org/cgi-bin/acts/acts_resolution.pl?resolution=2000-C025.

5. Panel discussion, "Social Visionary Panel: Domestic Violence Forum," Hood College, Frederick, Md., April 3, 2008.

6. *The Book of Common Prayer* (New York: Church Hymnal Corp., 1977), 305.

Chapter 1

Facts about Domestic Violence

DEFINING DOMESTIC VIOLENCE

My life is spent with sorrow, and my years with sighing; my strength fails because of my misery.

Psalm 31:10

Domestic violence is a pattern of coercive behavior characterized by the domination and control of one person over another, usually an intimate partner, through physical, psychological, emotional, verbal, sexual, and/or economic abuse. Examining this definition piece by piece is a helpful way to understand the complex ways abuse takes place:

a pattern—a predictable cycle of violence that repeats throughout the relationship.

of coercive behavior—Abusers often make up impossible rules and punish the victim for breaking them. They are manipulative and insist that they are always "right." They coerce their victims into feelings of guilt.

characterized by the domination and control of one person over another—Abusers seek to isolate their victims from family and friends. They may monitor phone calls, read mail, and insist on knowing where their victims are at all times. The need of the abuser to control his or her victim is the key factor in abusive relationships.

usually an intimate partner—Abusers often appear quite charming to those who don't know or haven't seen their abusive side and may lure their victims by highly attentive behavior. The reality is that the abuser and victim are often locked in an unhealthy relationship where real needs are distorted. "I need you, you need me" is a phrase used by abusers to cloud real issues of conflict.

through physical—An occasional slap or shove eventually leads to serious injury for most victims. According to the National Network to End Domestic Violence 2007 Domestic Violence and Assault Fact Sheet,[1] over 30% of women seen in emergency rooms are there because of domestic violence.

psychological—Abusers threaten to harm the victim, children in the household, family members, and pets, and they abuse the trust of the victim by using lies and exhibiting extreme jealousy.

emotional—Abusers tend to withhold feelings and complements, and they minimize the victim's opinions and concerns.

---

1.   www.nnedv.org/docs/Census/DVCounts2007DVCounts 07_Report_Color.pdf, "Domestic Violence Counts: 07: A 24-hour census of domestic violence shelters and services across the United States."

verbal—Abusers criticize, make humiliating remarks, yell, swear, mock, and use hurtful names to make the victim feel unworthy and unlovable.

sexual—Abusers may force sex on an unwilling partner and demand degrading or unwanted sexual acts.

and economic abuse—Abusers often refuse to give their victims money, and they may interfere with the victim's job or refuse to allow them to hold a job, prohibiting the victim from any independent choice over spending.

THE VICTIMS OF DOMESTIC VIOLENCE
My God, my God, why have you forsaken me?
Psalm 22:1

The victims of domestic violence include adults, children, the elderly, teens, college students—in short, anyone can be a victim of this crime. Although a 2006 U.S. Governmental Accountability Office report to Congress on the Prevalence of Domestic Violence notes that "perfect data may never exist because of the sensitive nature of these issues and the likelihood that all occurrences related to domestic violence . . . will not be disclosed,"[2] statistics collected by many reputable organizations corroborate the seriousness of this pervasive crime. These statistics summarize the cost of domestic violence to our communities, churches, and society. The following statistics are a compilation from various sources that appeared in *Now That the Silence is Broken*,[3] a 2002

2. GAO-07-148R Prevalence of Domestic Violence, 2006.

3. The Committee on the Status of Women, *Now That the Silence is Broken* (Cincinnati: Forward Movement Publications, 2002), 5–7.

publication from Forward Movement and the Women's Desk of the Episcopal Church.

Adults:
- Approximately 85–95% of the victims of domestic violence are women.
- Men are also abused, most often verbally and emotionally.
- More than 50% of all residential calls to which police respond are related to domestic violence.
- Approximately 81% of all abusers come from violent homes.
- Half of all homeless women and children are fleeing from domestic abuse.
- Approximately 4 women are murdered every day by their abusers.

Children and the Elderly:
- Between 50% and 70% of men who abuse their female partners also abuse children or elderly persons in the household.
- Children who grow up in an abusive household are learning to use abusive behavior and are more likely to become abusers or to enter abusive relationships.
- Children who witness domestic violence are at higher risk for suicide, substance abuse, truancy, and homelessness.
- Approximately 62% of sons over the age of 14 in abusive households, are injured when attempting to protect their mothers from attacks by male partners.
- Children are also at high risk of abuse from the victim, who feels heightened frustration and may strike out at the next weakest person in the household in order to try to restore a sense of control or power.

Teens and College Students:

- One-third of high school and college students experience violence in an intimate relationship during their dating years.
- Many young women, having been taught to be helpful and compassionate, become convinced that they can "save" their abusers and help them change. Nothing is further from the truth.
- Bullies and those who use intimidation at school are more likely to use it in the home as well.
- Victims of abuse are more likely to develop depression, anorexia, obesity, and self destructive behaviors in their teen and college years.

Families and Society:

- One out of every three families will experience episodes of domestic violence.
- Witnessing domestic violence is the single most accurate predictor of juvenile delinquency and adult criminality among young men.
- By the age of 18, the average youth in America will have watched 250,000 acts of violence and 40,000 attempted murders on television and in the movies.
- There are three times as many shelters for animals as there are for battered persons and their children.

THE CYCLE OF VIOLENCE

You therefore, beloved, since you are forewarned,
beware that you are not carried away with the error
of the lawless and lose your own stability.

2 Peter 3:17

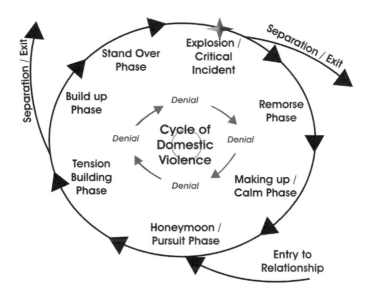

Understanding the cycle of violence is an important step
toward learning to prevent domestic violence and helping
those who are victims. Although the cycle has been illus-
trated in domestic violence literature since the early 1980s,
this illustration contains a different pattern, indicating both
entrance and exit ramps to show how persons may become
involved in the cycle, but offering hope by pointing out that
this is not a closed circle, doomed to repeat forever.

Each phase of the cycle may last for days, months, or years. There is no set pattern of time represented in the cycle of violence, only a repeated pattern of behavior. The characteristics listed are examples of the types of behaviors that may occur in each phase. A critical battering incident, for example, may last for minutes or hours. In extreme, but unfortunately not rare, domestic violence cases, the incident results in murder or murder/suicide.

Denial is the engine that keeps the cycle rolling. The batterer avoids responsibility, denying abuse or blaming the victim; the victim denies the real danger and tries to protect the relationship by minimizing or "forgetting" the violence; and both parties pretend that the incident is a one-time exception and will not happen again.

In most cases, the frequency of critical incidents increases, and the cool-down and build-up times shorten as the relationship continues. Over time, the cycle of violence comes to dominate the relationship, stifling the free expression of emotion and will on the part of the victim. The cycle of violence becomes habitual as the expectations of both persons become defined by the repeated pattern.

Phases of the Cycle of Violence

Honeymoon/Pursuit Phase: Many violent relationships begin with quick, intense, seductive courtships. The victim often looks back on this happy, loving time, hoping that the abuse will end and that the abuser will return to being the person he or she "once was." Memories of this phase and false expectations often prolong the abusive relationship.

Tension Building Phase: This phase is characterized by a gradual rise in tension, a building of threat, intimidation, or control and may last days, weeks, months, or even years.

Once set in motion, it will occur more frequently as the abuser becomes more demanding, jealous, and controlling. Victims begin to feel tense and afraid. They try to placate the abuser by becoming more and more compliant, even to the extent of giving up relationships with family and friends. When someone challenges the victim's behavior, he or she will defend the abuser, making excuses and minimizing events of conflict. Promises made during the calm or honeymoon phase begin to deteriorate. The abuser claims he or she is "cured" and doesn't need counseling or any other outside intervention that would lead to mutual responsibility.

Build up Phase: Tensions begin to reach a peak, and small incidents of abuse may occur. Blaming increases, and the victim continues to believe that if he or she just works hard enough or acts in the "right way," the tension will go away. Victims may describe this phase as "walking on eggshells."

Stand Over Phase: After a time, the victim is emotionally exhausted and detaches psychologically. The abuser, sensing the retreat, is more controlling and possessive, and monitors the victim's every move. The victim gives up trying to explain or justify her actions, as she feels that whatever she does or says is misinterpreted by the abuser. In nonviolent relationships, these tensions can be resolved, and many couples seek outside help. In violent relationships, the communication breaks down, and tensions eventually erupt into the next phase, the battering incident.

Explosion/Critical Incident Phase: At some point, there is a violent episode that involves physical abuse, destruction of property, and/or heightened emotional outbursts. Pets and children may be the first victims. During the first episode in this phase, minimal levels of violence may be enough to frighten the victim and discharge the abuser's fury.

As time goes on, however, more severe forms of abuse occur, and the abuser applies other methods of power and coercion. These methods may be so effective that in relationships where there is no physical form of abuse, victims may not even recognize they are in abusive relationships! Yet, there is almost always an escalation of abuse over time that corresponds to the erosion of the self-esteem of the one who is abused. Anxiety levels rise, and the abuser blames the victim. In many relationships, a critical incident can be the means by which abuse is exposed to family, friends, and outside authorities. The victim may have to be hospitalized, or the police, called to the residence. At this point, the victim often faces a choice: continue in the relationship, or find a way to separate or end the relationship. In tragic cases the critical incident may include the death of the victim and/or children at the hands of the abuser and/or the suicide of the abuser.

Abuse is more likely to occur when the abusers want to gain status in the eyes of others, to "prove their man hood" or "win the argument." They will continue intimidating the victim until they feel they have regained control over their environment, and the victim has backed down or retreated. At this point, they may boast to others about their power and control. Violence is more likely when the abuser feels a loss of self-esteem and seeks dominance over one with less power. This is a type of bullying. When the abuser feels loss of power in other areas of his or her life, such as economic loss or other conditions that cause stress, the person may seek to gain control over whoever is perceived as controllable—wife, girlfriend, child, pet. Substance abuse may also lead to a loss of inhibition that contributes to a violent outburst. However, none of these factors are a reason for or an excuse for domestic violence. There is no excuse for abuse.

Remorse Phase: Following a critical incident, the attitude of the abuser suddenly changes to one of remorse. The abuser may beg to be forgiven and offer promises to seek counseling, seeming to be shocked by the explosive incident. The abuser promises that "it will never happen again" or "I would never do anything to hurt you; I love you." The abuser denies responsibility and blames outside factors such as tension at work, substance abuse, or past traumas.

Making up/Calm Phase: During this phase there is a period of shock when the relationship goes "on hold." The abuse temporarily stops, and the abuser may seek help, join AA, go to church, or promise to attend counseling. The victim may take on the blame for the critical incident and feel obliged to forgive the abuser and remain in the relationship. Everyone is relieved that the crisis has passed; the victim is worn down and accepts promises that the abuser will change. The couple may draw in children as peacemakers or see them as the reason to keep the relationship together.

Honeymoon/Pursuit Phase: When the cycle has run its course and the relationship returns to the Honeymoon/Pursuit phase, it is tempting for victims to believe that the abuse has ended. Nothing is further from the truth because this is a still part of the repetitive cycle. This is the most deceptive and misunderstood phase of them all. When the relationship is in this phase, the victim may feel that the couple has returned to a more romantic stage of the relationship, and that he or she has managed to meet the needs of the abuser. The abuser may provide profuse apologies, gifts, and promises that abuse will never occur again. Both persons minimize and rationalize the abusive behavior and seriousness of any injuries. They may seek counseling and/ or renew their spiritual practices. Romance and sexual intimacy seem to heal all wounds and promise a false sense of security and resolution.

However, this is just the rewinding of the cycle of violence, and without intervention or radical change on the part of one or both persons in the abusive relationship, the cycle will repeat.

Separation/Exit Paths: The cycle of violence is not a closed circle; it has exit paths. The victim can leave the cycle at any point, but there are a few phases where leaving the violent relationship is more likely to occur with safety and success. One is directly after the explosion/critical incident in the case when abusers have been detained or incarcerated. Victims may obtain legal protection.

Victims and their children may also leave the home and move into a crisis shelter. During this time it is important for the victim to receive some kind of professional intervention. Due to the abuser's manipulative behavior, many victims are coerced into returning to their homes and allowing their abusers to return home as well, perpetuating rather than exiting the cycle.

Another common exit path occurs during the tension-building phase. This path is often charted and planned in advance with the help of local domestic violence programs, family, church, and law enforcement. Exiting the cycle of violence is most effective when it is multidimensional, making use of the aforementioned resources. Most domestic violence programs work in concert with law enforcement, social agencies, the legal system, the courts, and a victim's own family and faith community to help victims during the transition away from the cycle of violence and toward regaining self-respect and the ability to be a productive and positive member of society.

It is important to realize that the abuser will usually resist any idea of separation. The abusive personality is threatened by loss of control over the victim, the partner's independence, and the suggestion of separation from the tangled, abusive relationship. Due to their jealous and needy behaviors, abusers will act out and may resort to an escalation of abuse, while blaming it on their victim's bid for freedom.

The greatest time of danger for the victims is while they are in the process of leaving or directly after they have left an abusive relationship. The help of law enforcement and domestic violence programs can provide a more secure environment during separation. Many shelters are set up for maximum privacy and safety, not releasing their locations to the public and providing twenty-four hour supervision. The safety of any children present in the home is a serious consideration. Preparing a safety plan is the best way to minimize the danger during the couple's separation.

A Word About Forgiveness

The cycle of violence is a particular danger zone for those taught to practice the Christian virtues of *forgiveness* and *forbearance*. Abusers will use these words, and victims will believe that they are doing "what Jesus would do" only if they forgive the abuser and stay in the relationship. Abusers may even quote scriptures that seem to imply that a woman should "submit" to her spouse.

If they are married, the victims often feel it is up to them to make the marriage work, to prove to the family, the church, and to God that they can keep their marriage vows. Christian friends and even the church can unknowingly perpetuate the cycle of violence when they minimize behaviors, excuse outbursts, and believe the manipulative contrition of the abusers. During the honeymoon phase, the abuser may try to convince his or her victim to forgive, but will take no accountability for the actions of abuse.

Forgiveness is a process, not just a one-time action. True forgiveness typically comes later, after a victim has broken free of the coercive behavior and can think and choose what course is best. Forgiveness does not release the abuser from responsibility. It is a healing process for the victim *after* a sense of safety and self-worth has been regained

MYTHS AND REALITIES
Contend, O Lord, with those who contend with me; fight against those who flight against me!

Psalm 35:1

Many myths abound that serve to perpetuate the victimization of those in abusive relationships. These myths are the result of misunderstandings about domestic violence as well as the instinctive avoidance most people feel when faced with unpleasant subjects. Some myths are perpetuated by abusers to manipulate their victims, while others have come from entrenched cultural stereotypes. Exploring these myths can contribute to a heightened sense of concern and encourage people of conscience to assist victims.

Myth: Domestic violence only happens in poor families or in cases of drug or alcohol abuse.
Reality: While substance abuse can lower inhibitions, it is not the cause of domestic violence. There are just as many abused women living in higher economic brackets as there

are abused women living in poverty. In reality, victims who are better educated and more privileged may be able to hide the abuse more effectively and be less likely to receive the help they need.

Myth: Domestic violence is only physical abuse that results in visible bruises.
Reality: Physical violence is part of a larger pattern of emotional and psychological coercion by which an abuser uses a variety of methods to keep control of the relationship. Men are more likely to be victims of emotional abuse and may not recognize it as domestic violence because it lacks a physical component. Women who are accused of physically abusing their partners may be fighting back in defense against stronger abusers.

Myth: If the abuser is truly sorry and promises to reform, the abuse will stop.
Reality: Remorse and begging are part of the cycle of violence and are a method of control. Without intervention and counseling, few abusers will take responsibility for their actions.

Myth: The victim can always walk away from the relationship.
Reality: Domestic violence counselors report that by the time most victims leave an abusive situation, they have tried to leave more than ten times before. Victims believe that they do not have any place to go where they will be safe from the abuser. The abuser often knows and is known by the victim's friends and relatives. The abusers use fear and intimidation as weapons if the victim tries to leave, and abusers often strip the victim of money, independence, and self-esteem.

Myth: The abuser just has a "bad temper," and the victim is to blame for not trying hard enough to be pleasant and loving.
Reality: Abusers often blame the abused for "making them angry" or "making them lose control." Victims are usually placed in a "no win" situation where no amount of trying will ever placate the abuser. Experts agree that "anger management" is not an effective response to abusers who are able to contain their anger in public situations. They do not assault their bosses, ministers, or neighbors, just their intimate partners.

Myth: When a child is a bully, he is just expressing his immature "natural" anger: "boys will be boys," and "the girls had it coming."
Reality: Bullying is abuse in its infancy. Bullies are often abused at home, and their behavior is excused and even encouraged as a natural expression of aggression, manliness, or assertiveness. Adults must defend children who are the victims of bullies and not expect them to cope on their own. Bullies must be given strict boundaries for their behavior, held to specific behaviors, and be separated from potential victims by a responsible adult. Unfortunately, the parents of bullies will not usually recognize the seriousness of their children's behavior, as they are often using the same behavior in the home.

Myth: Men who batter may still be good fathers and should have joint custody of the children if the couple separates.
Reality: The patterns of control and intimidation often continue after separation, and many studies reveal that men who batter their wives also abuse their children. Children suffer from being put in the middle of a dysfunctional relationship.

Myth: Once a battered person, always a battered person.

Reality: People who receive appropriate intervention, assistance, and counseling can, in time, regain their self-image and create a stable and productive life. They can also learn about healthy relationships and make better choices in the future.

Myth: Those with strong religious beliefs will not become batterers or are less likely to be abused.

Reality: Religious beliefs or affiliations do not prevent someone from being battered. Some victims feel their religious beliefs help them to endure the violence. Abusers may use religious beliefs to falsely justify their behaviors or as threats, intimidation, or guilt against those they are abusing. The church and religious leaders may unknowingly present concepts of sacrifice, forgiveness, and service in such a way that creates vulnerability for well-meaning persons. Teaching about marriage, divorce, gender roles, and family dynamics must emphasize mutual respect and nonviolent behavior as essential components of healthy Christian relationships.

Chapter 2

The Role of Religion

WHY THE CHURCH HAS REMAINED SILENT
Many are saying to me, "there is no help for you in
God."

Psalm 3:2

Domestic violence is everywhere. Even in a close-knit
church community, there may be individuals who are
experiencing or have experienced domestic violence, and
there may be no outward signs. Far-reaching studies cited
throughout this book show that there are persons in every
group, every culture, and every socioeconomic stratum
who are abused.

Although we may realize that abuse does occur, the
church may feel immobilized and reluctant to act because
we so highly value the sacrament of marriage and the holiness of the family. What are the barriers to addressing the
issue of domestic violence in religious settings and congregations? Our support of marriage may cause us to assume
that most problems will cure themselves and that most inci-
dences of abuse are isolated.

In the Episcopal marriage service, the congregation is asked, "Will all of you witnessing these promises do all in your power to uphold these two persons in their marriage?" The reply is, "We will." To do "all in our power" is to make a pledge of involvement and support for the individuals, not just the institution of marriage.

Recognizing the barriers to action is the first step towards overcoming them. Following are some common assumptions that act as barriers for laity and clergy, coupled with corresponding realities that encourage action and response to begin breaking the silence.[1]

Assumption: Domestic violence is not occurring in any families in our church.

Fact: Statistics compiled by national domestic violence agencies consistently show that domestic violence takes place in the homes of families in every social and economic class and that 26%, or up to 1 in 4, women in America are abused at some point in their lives, affecting 28% of all marriages. The issue is not if but who. Part of the problem is that those who are abused are fearful and ashamed. Silence is a major part of the pattern of abuse. If the church provides a safe environment, victims may disclose their pain, but the fact that no one is talking about problems in the home is not an indication that abuse is not occurring in the households of your church.

Assumption: The church should not invade the privacy of the family.

Fact: The church has long supported teachings and practices that directly influence family behaviors when it comes

---

1. This chapter is adapted from *Breaking the Wall of Silence: Domestic Violence Prevention and the Congregation* by Louisa Page (Cambridge, Mass.: Episcopal Divinity School), 2001.

to birth, illness, divorce, death, and the use of resources of time, talent, and treasure. The church responds, often without being directly asked or invited, when someone is ill, hospitalized, or homebound. Privacy and confidentiality are part of the clerical vows that ministers exercise to protect members with vulnerable issues and assist them in making healthy and beneficial choices.

Assumption: Abuse is primarily between adults and will not necessarily affect the children.

Fact: Often the victims most hurt in abusive families are the children. Children who grow up in violent households are more likely to become violent and carry on the legacy of abuse to a new generation. They are likely to become victims of the abuser, and in some cases even the adult victim abuses the children in an attempt to gain control over an uncontrollable situation, or neglects them due to stress, fear, and exhaustion. Studies have found that abuse is a learned behavior and that violence in the home is a predictor of criminal behavior and delinquency in teen-age years.

Assumption: Marriage vows are sacred, and marriage should be preserved at all costs.

Fact: While sacred, vows do not guarantee the behavior of the individual. When abuse is taking place, the covenant of love and mutual affection that the vows establish is violated, and the marriage is in danger of being destroyed. Pretending that the vows alone will somehow protect both the abuser and the abused does nothing to help both individuals honor one another and their promise to God. The Episcopal marriage canons and the governing documents of other major Christian denominations acknowledge that the priority in cases of marital stress is the safety of the persons involved and that when abuse is taking place, the dissolution of the marriage is an option.

Assumption: The harm that is taking place is probably exaggerated.

Fact: Both the abused and the abuser will tend to minimize rather than exaggerate the extent of the harm and violence that are taking place. The abused are usually fearful, intimidated, and ashamed to admit when domestic violence is occurring. They may not want to recognize or reveal to their church friends or minister that their marriage is less than ideal. The abusers, when confronted, typically minimize their behavior as justifiable and make excuses blaming stress, normal difficulties, and misunderstandings. They will characterize abuse as a one-time outburst. If abuse is suspected, it is probably occurring.

Assumption: A minister should not "take sides" between two parishioners because the minister is called to serve all.

Fact: By failing to respond, the minister is taking the side of the abuser. By failing to raise the issue of domestic violence and to provide instruction and information about its characteristics and effects, the church ignores the harm to the larger community. Addressing the issue may help those who are potential victims learn to recognize the signs of abusive relationships before they are caught up in a cycle of violence. When abuse is suspected, experts strongly urge ministers to refer a couple to a counselor trained in domestic violence issues. Triangulation is a manipulative tactic that abusers employ to keep ministers at a distance and to avoid healthy confrontation and responsibility. When a minister attempts to remain impartial, there is always the tendency to try to lend equal credence to the husband and the wife. In cases of domestic abuse, the victim will be reluctant to express the true extent of the abuse, and the abuser will tend to justify their actions. The minister will be caught in the denial of both parties, while not improving the situation between them.

Assumption: A local congregation lacks the training or expertise to effectively help victims of domestic violence.
Fact: While this may initially be true, effective help begins with awareness, with making appropriate resources and referrals available, and with the refusal to remain silent. Training programs are available from local domestic violence programs, and most church structures on regional and national levels have trained leaders who will come, when invited, to lead workshops or meet with church groups. Resources exist in every community, and the World Wide Web has numerous sites that offer help.

Assumption: The issue of domestic violence is a legal and political one, outside the direct domain of the church.
Fact: Domestic violence damages the spirit of the abused and the abuser. The church is called to "set captives free" from the control of sin and death. Domestic violence results in the death of women in every state and community, every town, city, and village. According to a National Poll conducted by the Allstate Foundation on Domestic Violence in 2004 and quoted on the website of the National Domestic Violence Hotline, 3 out of 4 (74%) respondents personally know someone who is or has been a victim of domestic violence.[2] The church as the body of Christ is called to serve the "least of these" (Matt 25:45). How humans treat one another is one of the greatest witnesses to the power of Christ's Gospel of hope, love, and life.

---

2. http://www.ndvh.org/educate/abuse_in_america.html.

Assumption: Male preeminence is sanctioned by scripture and church tradition.

Fact: There are no Biblical references to gender that advocate or condone violence as a way of maintaining control of one person over another in an intimate relationship. Men who abuse women often believe in an extreme stereotype of male/female roles and twist scripture to fit their preconceived notions. Mutual agreement or vows that form marriage do not erase the commandment to love your neighbor as yourself, or the "golden rule" to do unto others as you would have them do unto you. Jesus' greatest and last commandment was to love one another as he loved us. Although America's constitution upholds the separation of church and state, abuse is never a protected religious right. It is a moral wrong and a legal crime.

Assumption: Interpersonal violence is the result of the sinful nature of humans. It has always existed, and the congregation has only limited power to influence what is an individual responsibility.

Fact: Perpetrators of abuse need the silence of a community in order to pursue their destructive behavior. A community of faith can create a place of safety where the victims can seek help and protection. A community message that challenges destructive behavior may limit abuse or in the best of circumstances guide abusers into admitting their responsibility and seeking help to end their destructive behavior. Victims who hear consistent messages of hope and affirmation learn options and paths out of the cycle of violence.

CHURCH HISTORY AND DOMESTIC VIOLENCE

Hear my cry, O God; listen to my prayer.

Psalm 61:1

The church must come to grips with theological teaching and historical practices that for thousands of years have condoned both men abusing their wives and the larger abuse of women in the western "Christian" society. According to Susan Brooks Thistlethwaite in her 1981 address to the Minnesota Governor's Conference on the Church and Battered Women, the roots of spouse abuse lie deeply imbedded in the religious belief that women are to be subject to men. The church must actively reexamine a series of long-standing teachings that trace the subjugation of women to the interpretation of the story of the Creation and the Fall found in Genesis chapters 1–2. In the New Testament the Apostle Paul cites Genesis and Eve's responsibility for the fall as justification for keeping women silent in the church (1 Timothy 2:12–14). This interpretation of Genesis provided an undergirding for a patriarchal authority that was considered ordained by God for most of the history of the church as supported by some of the greatest theologians. St. Augustine, in his classic work *The City of God*, interprets the Fall as due entirely to feminine fault. He asserts that woman's subordinate role is a punishment for her guilt in causing evil to come into the world, leading to the death of Christ. Thomas Aquinas' treatise *Summa Theologia* relies on Aristotle's view that "woman is defective and misbegotten . . ." and must be ruled over by the man, who embodies a reasonable force, for the good order of the family.

According to Rosemary Radford Ruether in an address to the Governor's Conference on Battered Women in 1980, the literature of the church throughout the middle ages allowed men to beat their wives and justified physical violence against women who were always seen as "asking for it" or deserving it. Ruether quotes G. G. Coulton's "Women's Life" from *Medieval Panorama* on the duties of upper class society regarding a story of a wife who rebukes her husband in public. He strikes her to the floor with his fist and breaks her nose with his foot, thereby leaving a permanent mark on her face. The book holds this story up as a "good lesson" for women regarding what they ought to expect if they cross their husbands. In St. Thomas More's *Utopia*, a book about an ideal society, husbands are depicted as chastising their wives and the wives, as ministering to their husbands in all things, falling prostrate at their feet, and begging forgiveness if they have offended in any way.

During the Reformation, Martin Luther and other religious leaders did little to reconstruct these traditional interpretations. Luther maintained that Eve was the primarily guilty party of the Fall while Adam went along with her but was relatively innocent. Eve's guilt is deepened in that she broke God's law. Ruether explains that the later reformers stayed in this theological strain. When a woman wrote to John Calvin requesting help in leaving her abusive husband, he replied:

We have a special sympathy for poor women who are evilly and roughly treated by their husbands, because of the roughness and cruelty of the tyranny and captivity which is their lot. We do not find ourselves permitted by the Word of God, however, to advise a woman to leave her husband, except by force of necessity; and we do not understand this force to be operative when a husband behaves roughly and uses threats to his wife, nor ever when he beats her, but [only] when there is imminent peril to her life, whether from persecutions by the husband or by his conspiring . . . [W]e . . . exhort her to bear with patience the cross which God has seen fit to place upon her; and meanwhile not to deviate from the duty which she has before God to please her husband, but to be faithful whatever happens.

This literalistic Biblicism persists today among many churches and among a cultural understanding of Christianity that permeates American society. Even women and men who do not attend or are not members of a church know something about the tradition that subjugates women to men and makes the marriage vow a binding chain in cases of abuse. Those who work with victims of domestic violence report that women who seek counseling and shelter feel that they have failed God and are sinful for wanting to break their marriage vows. They may feel that they were not able to do their duty as wives and have not been able to "carry the cross" that God has given them. In some cases, their own ministers have counseled them to forgive their husbands who beat them, as Christ forgave those who crucified him.

Women with violent spouses have often believed that the Bible actually says what they have heard or been taught it says—that women are inferior in status to their husbands and God and that they deserve a life of pain. A woman may believe that it is God's will that she continue to suffer and that her suffering may in some way eventually change the behavior of her husband. She may believe that breaking her marriage vows is a greater sin than the abuse she receives. She may believe that her husband is a broken soul in need of patience and forbearance. She may believe that she is "blessed" when she is "meek" and interpret meekness as acceptance of her inferior status. She may believe that as long as she attends church with her husband, there is a chance that he will change and love her in the same way she sees other "Christian" husbands loving their wives. There is a double bind for women in the Christian tradition, implying that when they are abused they have "asked for it" and therefore do not deserve the mercy, understanding, or protection of the church, and that the church will not restrain or rebuke their abusers.

In today's society, the church must reclaim the gospel of hope and reteach the words of the Bible in light of interpretive methods that have been broadly used for over a hundred years. Many churches have vigorously embraced methods that place words of the Bible in their historical context while recognizing the eternal truths expressed by authoritative scripture. Anyone may use these methods—even non-Christians—to better understand the larger picture of the Christian approach and may help liberate the thinking of women who are abused and men who justify their abuse on religious grounds.

GUIDELINES FOR INTERPRETING SCRIPTURE[3]

There are some things in [Paul's writings] . . . hard to understand, which the ignorant and unstable twist to their own destruction, as they do the other scriptures. . . . But grow in the grace and knowledge of our Lord and Savior Jesus Christ.

2 Peter 3:16, 18a

---

3. This chapter is adapted from Ellen F. Davis and Richard B. Hays, "Beyond Criticism: Learning to Read the Bible Again," *The Christian Century*, April 20, 2004; http://findarticles.com/p/articles/mi_m1058/is_8_121/ai_n6003108/pg_6Beyond criticism: learning to read the Bible again.

The Bible is not a novel, nor is it a "cookbook" for moral behavior. Theologians have sometimes said it is more like a love letter from God to humanity. It is actually a complex set of separate books, more like a library under one cover that multiple authors have written over a period of several thousand years. The final compilation of the books of the Bible took place several hundred years after the beginning of the Common Era (CE), and the divisions of chapter and verse were added hundreds of years later. The Old Testament was written in Hebrew and Aramaic, and the New Testament was originally written in Greek. Both Testaments were translated into Latin during the middle ages. It was only during the Reformation that the Bible was translated into the languages of various countries—English, German, French. Thus any English version is a translation, using the best equivalents of concepts that do not always directly correspond to English words.

The Bible contains different kinds of literature: history, poetry, prophecy, proverbs, and parables. It is full of metaphors such as the words attributed to Jesus: "I am the gate for the sheep" (John 10:7). This does not mean that Jesus is literally a gate, but that his love is *like* an entrance or place of safety. Jesus uses metaphors in his many parables that begin, "The kingdom of God is *like* . . . ." Interpretation of scripture was taking place even at the time when Jesus' words were being recorded. Take for example the parable of the seed found in Matthew, chapter 13. The parable is delivered, and then a few verses later is an explanation of the meaning. While a full study of Biblical interpretation is far beyond the scope of this book, there are a few guidelines that anyone may use to help those who feel trapped by the misuse of God's Word.

We are to understand scripture within the context of the overarching story of God's love. While the Bible contains many contradictions and tensions, the texts are coherent because the belief in one God lies behind them. Any single verse of scripture cannot be understood or used in isolation but must be laid against other similar or contradictory texts, keeping in mind the large themes that lie behind the collection of writings. For example, the theme of God's Covenant of love with humanity is woven throughout the Old Testament, then appears in the New Testament embodied in Jesus Christ—the fulfillment of the Covenant. Disregarding the theme and using one verse of scripture to justify a certain behavior violates the broader meaning of the Bible.

Texts of scripture do not have a single meaning limited by previous interpretations. Faithful reading of scripture invites us to dip again and again into the meanings that God reveals in new times and new places. For example, the requirement from Paul that women cover their heads is largely understood as a cultural response for the times and not to be carried on as a requirement in most churches.

The people in the community of faith provide guidance in how to interpret and respond to the teachings of scripture. Even loyal critics may open up information that adds to the collected tradition of the church. Those whom the church considered "saints" demonstrate the power of scripture in the virtues of their lives and in the manner in which they love and serve others. For example, Christians living in pre-World War II Europe felt it was their duty to resist the laws of the Nazi party and shelter Jews in their homes, even though some scriptures imply Christians should be subject to the laws of the state.

One needs to read the scriptures in dialog with diverse communities outside the church. Reading the scripture with Jewish scholars in particular will provide many insights into the world in which Jesus was born and lived as a pious Jew.

For example, the Passover meal still celebrated by Jews contains many rituals that for Christians seem to point to Jesus' death and resurrection.

The Bible is a narrative based on the lives of those who were called to worship and follow God, who calls us into relationship in the context of human history. The historic time of Jesus and Paul, Moses and Isaiah, was different from the present day, with its own set of cultural expectations and assumptions. This is particularly true when examining the role of women in a society that was, especially in the Old Testament, patriarchal and polygamous. For example, almost all Christians today believe that monogamy is God's will, even though the faith's patriarchs—Abraham, Isaac, and Jacob—lived very differently.

The story and work of God is not done. Christians affirm that Jesus Christ will come again and that we live in a time in between the breaking forth of the Kingdom of God in the life, death, and resurrection of Jesus Christ, and the completion of God's reign on earth. Sin and hate are still present realities, and we are called as people of "water and the spirit" to work for justice and seek God's forgiveness within the context of the time and place in which we live.

Are the words on the page sacred in and of themselves? Or is the way the words are used and understood what makes them authoritative and sacred? Do the words have intrinsic value, or is the value of words made known as they are heard by the human soul and lived out in real life? Different Christian communities of faith will express the authority of the Bible according to their history and tradition, but those who misuse the scripture will tend to focus narrowly on their own perspective of the words, and miss the larger meaning and context of this collection of sacred writings.

TEXTS OF WOMEN ABUSED

Fear and trembling come upon me, and horror overwhelms me. And I say, "O that I had wings like a dove! I would fly away and be at rest. . . . I would hurry to find a shelter for myself from the raging wind and tempest.

Psalm 55:5–8

Domestic violence has some roots in spiritual abuse. Spiritual abuse is misusing the power of sacred texts, church tradition, or sacramental authority (including that of ordained leaders) to oppress or victimize. For centuries, abusers have misused sacred texts to justify their actions and keep the oppressed in their control. The following is a brief journey into some of the Biblical texts that have contributed to the misunderstanding of God's gospel of love, peace, and reconciliation.

In 1984 theologian Phyllis Trible wrote a book called *Texts of Terror: Literary-Feminist Readings of Biblical Narratives*. In the Introduction she writes, "In this book my task is to tell sad stories. . . . They are tales of terror with women as victims. . . . If art imitates life, scripture likewise reflects it in both holiness and horror . . . yet by enabling insight, [reflections] may inspire repentance. In other words, sad stories may yield new beginnings."[4]

Entering into study of these stories may unlock old memories and more recent anxieties. Women especially may identify with the reality that all of us learn at one time or another from our mothers, sisters, or peers—some men are dangerous. We may remember the "wolf whistle" from the street, the instant fear when facing a dark parking lot, and the shame of being teased about our appearance or

---

4.   (Philadelphia: Fortress Press, 1984), 1–2.

sexuality. The following are not just stories about people who lived long ago in less civilized societies. Like all of Holy Scripture, they are authoritative for the church; they hold mysteries and messages that we hear differently as we read them again and again, at different times in our lives. Churches and their leaders may differ on the exact interpretation and use of these passages. What follows is not offered as a definitive pronouncement but as an opportunity to challenge and uncover our own subtle prejudices and preconceptions. Likewise, this study may serve as a reassuring word to those whose lives have been oppressed by spiritual abuse.

The Rape of Tamar: 2 Samuel 13:1–22[5]

This tale of terror is part of the larger narrative about King David and is found within the story of Absalom, David's beloved and doomed son, third in line to the throne behind Amnon and Chileab (2 Samuel 3:3). It follows the more familiar passage of lust, adultery, and murder involving David's affair with Bathsheba, mother of Solomon. Tamar was Absalom's full sister, but half sister to Amnon. Throughout this narrative, Tamar is surrounded by men who determine her actions—her father, King David; her half-brother, Amnon, who desires her; her brother Absalom, who later avenges her; and Amnon's friend Jonadab, who plots the scene of seduction and rape.

The story begins as Amnon confesses his desire for Tamar and tries to convince her to "lie with him." Tamar does what she can to convince Amnon to follow the protocol of asking David to bed her legally. She resists when she

---

5. For a complete exegesis of this text, refer to *Texts of Terror* or the notes in any study Bible.

can, reminding Amnon that "such a thing is not done in Israel; [so] do not do anything so vile!" (vs. 12). She knows that once violated, her status as virgin daughter of a powerful king, and thus potential consort for a neighboring royal family, is ended. The scene that follows is full of signs of seduction. Amnon, pretends to be so sick he cannot rise from his bed. Following his friend Jonadab's advice, he asks his father, King David, to send Tamar to tend to him in his house. Tamar arrives, and Amnon requests that she come and prepare bread in his presence and feed him with her own hand. He then dismisses all the servants. Tamar is thus isolated and physically within reach of a larger and stronger person. Amnon watches as she works the dough, a sensuous image. He then overpowers Tamar and rapes her. Following this abuse, Amnon views Tamar as an object of loathing greater than the lust he had felt for her (vs. 15). He throws her out and attempts to distance himself from his own actions. He takes no responsibility while Tamar tears her clothes, puts ashes on her head, and goes away, crying, in the traditional posture of extreme mourning. For the rest of her days, Tamar is known as a "desolate woman" (vs. 20).

Women who live with abuse, or even those who have at one time or another felt fear when in a vulnerable position or environment, will recognize elements of their own experience in this story. Tamar is isolated from those who could protect her or from witnesses who might corroborate her story. Her abuser views her as an object with no right to say "no." She tries to reason with Amnon and seek a legitimate and appropriate way for him to behave. She responds to Amnon's apparent weakness and goes to his home to help him. She is overpowered by someone stronger. Once abused, her feelings are discounted and ignored. Beyond the family dysfunction is a story of lust and rejection that rings true today for all who feel like "desolate women."

The Unnamed Concubine: Judges 19:1–30

This story is located near the end of the book of Judges and takes place when the system of tribal leadership, in place since the Hebrews entered the "Promised Land," was disintegrating. Without a king to centralize authority, the tribes jostle for position. A certain Levite takes a woman of Bethlehem as his concubine. The story explains the origins of a tribal war against the Benjamities who were so thoroughly defeated by the Israelites that only a few survived. Beneath this tale of tribal warfare is a story of extreme abuse. The woman, a concubine, is something more than a slave, as she addresses the Levite as "husband," and her father is titled "father-in-law." But she is less than a wife, as the Levite is referred to as her "master."

The story opens as the concubine, who has become angry with the Levite, returns to her father's home in Bethlehem (the same city where Jesus is later born). The Levite sets out to get her to return to him, resolving to "speak tenderly" to her. The woman's father welcomes him and persuades him to stay for a few days. As the days go by and the Levite prepares to leave to take the concubine back home, the father persuades him to stay yet another day and another. This goes on for five days until the Levite refuses the father's offer of hospitality and leaves at the end of the day—not the usual time for departing on a long trip.

That evening as the day is drawing to a close, the traveling party stops in a place called Gibeah, a city belonging to the tribe of Benjamin. They go to the square of the city, hoping to find someone who will take them in for the night. An old man meets them and offers them shelter. But as the story progresses, a mob of men from the city surrounds the house and demands that the Levite yield himself to them. The old man who is hosting the travelers offers his virgin daughter and the concubine, but the mob does not listen. The Levite then pushes the concubine out the door, and the mob proceeds to rape and abuse her all night. As dawn breaks, the men let her go, and she makes her way back to the locked door of the house. When the master gets up in the morning, he finds her dead on the doorstep, with her hands on the threshold. We might imagine that with the last of her strength, the concubine had tried to open the door. The story ends as the Levite, outraged at the violation of his property, cuts the body of the concubine in pieces and sends them as evidence to the far corners of Israel. This results in a tribal war, and the book of Judges closes in chaos.

It is clear from what we know of this time in history that women were often counted as property to be owned and controlled. An interesting detail of this story is the fact that the woman had left her "husband" and when he came to get her, the father-in-law kept delaying his departure. Could it be that the daughter had informed him of abuse and had sought shelter in her ancestral home? The story further reveals sexual rape as a violent tool of hostility toward strangers, the opposite of the hospitality that was the expectation in that culture.[6] Women who have experienced domestic violence and who have left abusive relationships may recognize the pattern of the Levite who resolved to "speak tenderly" in order to bring her back. The protection her father offered was temporary in nature and did not prevail. Whether she returned to the Levite of her own free will or as a result of the Levite's "tender" words we

---

6. Some interpretations have used this story as one to condemn homosexual behavior because of their demand to "know" the Levite, "know" being a sexual reference. However, if the mob was intent on homosexual sex, the old man would not have offered the virgin daughter and concubine as a substitute, and the mob would not have abused the concubine.

will never know. Certainly, his tender words were nowhere to be found when he turned her over to the hostile men, offering no protection, remorse, or respect, even after her death. This account is an example of the cycle of violence in action. It begins with the "honeymoon" period, progresses through the "tension-building" phase, and ends with a critical incident and the murder of the abused woman.

TEXTS OF VICTIMS PROTECTED AND ABUSE EXPOSED

[Boaz said to Ruth,] "May the Lord reward you for your deeds, and may you have a full reward from the Lord, the God of Israel, under whose wings you have come for refuge!"

Ruth 2:12

Susanna: The Apocrypha

Perhaps a less familiar story of a woman victimized is found in the book of Susanna in the Apocrypha.[7] The event takes place during the Exile in Babylon. In this tale, Daniel, a familiar Biblical personage, practices the prophetic and leadership skills that later bring him to the attention of the king of Babylon. The king makes him a trusted advisor, incurring the jealousy of others who plot to get rid of him in the famous "lion's den" story from the book of Daniel. The tale of Susanna has all the familiar elements of abuse,

---

7. The Apocrypha refers to the 15 books present in the Greek version of the Old Testament, known as the Septuagint. These texts were written just prior to the first century, and many of the early church fathers called them authoritative. The Revised Common Lectionary uses selections from some of them. For a more complete explanation, you may refer to a Bible dictionary or other resource.

but this time the intentions of the abusers are thwarted, and Susanna is protected.

Susanna's story takes place within the Jewish community in exile in Babylon. Although the people of God were living in an alien culture, there is no opportunity given in the story to blame the improper behavior on the customs of outsiders. From the beginning of this account, the two elders of the Hebrew people who lust after Susanna, a virtuous wife of a trusted rich leader named Joakim, are depicted as evil. The two elders are judges, appointed to govern the people in exile according to their ethnic and religious laws. The court of law is hosted at the home of Joakim, where Susanna appears daily to take a walk in the garden. The two elders separately begin to lust for her, and when each eventually learns of the other's desire, they form a plot to seduce her.

The opportunity comes the next day when Susanna, thinking that the garden is empty, goes to take a bath, asking her servants to shut the garden doors. The two elders are hidden nearby, and once Susanna is isolated, they demand that she submit to them, or they will say she sent her maids away because she was meeting a young man. Susanna groans and admits that she is trapped between being accused of adultery, which carries a death sentence, or rape, which means eternal dishonor. Her words of refusal are reminiscent of Joseph's refusal to be seduced by the Pharaoh's wife (Genesis 39:9). She refuses their advances and begins to scream. One of the judges runs to open the garden doors (making it appear as if they have just rushed in), and the household servants arrive. As the elders tell their lie the household servants feel ashamed, "for nothing like this had ever been said about Susanna" (vs. 27, NRSV).

The next day when the elders arrive to hold court, they send for Susanna. She arrives with her parents, her children, and all her relatives. The elders try to humiliate her by requiring her to be unveiled, the equivalent of being stripped in public. They lay their hands on her head and claim they saw her embracing a young man in her garden. Because of their position of authority, the assembly believes their lie and condemns Susanna to death.

Susanna cries out to the Lord, and as she is being led away for execution, Daniel hears her and shouts, "I want no part in shedding this woman's blood!" (vs. 46). The procession stops, and Daniel convinces the people to return to court to learn the facts. The court is reconvened. Daniel separates the two evil elders and questions them, asking them to identify the type of tree under which they saw Susanna embracing the young man. Their differing testimony quickly exposes their lie and exonerates Susanna. The two elders are put to death.

This situation shows some elements that are present in any abusive setting. The elements of secrecy, falsehood, and denial are demonstrated by the behavior of the elders. They use their power, gender, and status, knowing they will be believed and Susanna will not. This abuse of power gains them temporary victory and silences Susanna. Even the servants, who feel shame at Susanna's behavior, are part of a system that blames the victim, believing that the marriage vow has been violated. They uphold the vow at the expense of the individual and without supporting the right of the wife to be heard.

The factors that save Susanna are the same that can serve to give direction and hope to victims of domestic violence. Susanna refuses to be silent and isolated. She screams for help. She calls upon her family, who rallies in force to support her. She tells the truth and continues to tell it until someone listens. She refuses to collude with denial and falsehood or believe what others say about her. She refuses to accept the shame of the servants who give up on her. One person in the community of faith steps forward to "hear" Susanna. He is inspired by the Holy Spirit and refuses to go along with the conventional judgment. He takes "his stand among them" (vs. 48) and defends the victim. The community responds, and Susanna is saved.

The Woman Taken in Adultery: John 8:1–11

Many have used this story from the Gospel of John to show Jesus' compassion toward women of his day and the exceptional way he dealt with them. The circumstances of the woman's life are unrevealed except for the fact that she is accused of adultery. The officials who bring her to Jesus make her stand before all of them and recite the conventional law of death for those caught in the act of adultery. They then ask Jesus, "Now what do you say?" (8:5) The Gospel writer reveals that their motivation is to trap Jesus. At first, Jesus says nothing and writes something on the ground. Then his reply is the now famous line, "Let anyone among you who is without sin be the first to throw a stone at her." When the crowd fades away, he turns and addresses the woman directly, asking her where her accusers are. When she replies, he states that he does not condemn her and sends her on her way, directing her not to sin again.

The elements of abuse in this incident are revealed by the power of the men who physically compel the woman to stand alone and exposed in the middle of a hostile crowd. She is isolated, pre-condemned, shamed, and defenseless. The religious officials have abused their power over her to make her a tool in their attempt to discredit Jesus. She is voiceless, unnamed, and silent. To them she is a non-person, an "it," already dead, and of no account or value except to trick Jesus without her consent or will.

Jesus responds in a fashion that is a hallmark of his entire ministry. He does not play into the setup, but he acts on his own and waits until the motivations of the accusers are revealed. His statement reminds those in the crowd that they must take responsibility for their own thoughts and actions. When the crowd melts away, Jesus turns to the woman and speaks to her, honoring her by his attentiveness and compassion. He does not automatically assume anything, but respects her story as she tells it. Jesus believes her, and he sends her on her way with encouragement and support.

HOW TO USE THESE STORIES
AS TEACHING TOOLS

All scripture is inspired by God and is useful for teaching, for reproof, for correction, and for training in righteousness, so that everyone who belongs to God may be proficient, equipped for every good work.

2 Timothy 3:16–17

These stories from the Bible may be used with small groups to help identify the signs of abuse and the response of the faith community to those who are victims. Exercise care to provide an environment that is supportive and safe, with the assumption that there will be persons in the room who will personally identify with the victims in these stories and may possibly recall painful events. Set norms of respect and confidentially before engaging in this study, and prepare leaders beforehand to recognize the characteristics of domestic violence, using the material in this book or equivalent resources. Use this commentary as a guideline for the following Bible study:

1. Lead the group in prayer, asking God for the guidance and protection of the Holy Spirit.

2. Before reading the stories from the Bible, ask the group members what they may already know or assume about the story—the people, the plot, the ending. Make it clear that the objective of the study is to learn more about domestic violence and its effects and ways the faith community might respond.

3. Read the story aloud in several translations, noting the variations. Identify the people, the plot line, and the turning points in the story. Note any emotional reactions of the participants. Are they shocked? Surprised?

4. Using the materials in this book that illustrate the cycle of violence or the characteristics of abuse, ask the group to list the elements of abuse in the story. (Check the preceding commentary.) Discuss. Have any group members ever felt that they have experienced the same elements? Are they willing to tell their stories?

5. Invite the group to list the elements of hope in the story. Who defended the victim? How did the community respond? Who was silent? Who stood up for the rights of the person involved? What options did the victim have (if any)?

6. Discuss. How does this story illustrate the issue of domestic abuse? What elements of the cycle of violence are present? Why was the victim able or not able to respond in her own defense? What elements of power demanded silence or conventional action? What helped to break that silence?

7. If there is time, turn to the section in this book about the response of the faith community. What actions

are already present in your setting? What responses might the group be willing to act upon?

8. End with prayer, using one of the forms given in chapter 5 of this book or another appropriate prayer.

THE HOLINESS OF MARRIAGE—MUTUAL REGARD
Husbands, love your wives, just as Christ loved the church and gave himself up for her.

Ephesians 5:25

Paul's letter to the church in Ephesus contains a section about the Christian household. Within that passage in the fifth chapter is a section that has become a tool for those seeking justification for their abusive actions in marriage. The difficulty lies in the misinterpretation of the word "subject." Paul describes a household of his own day with the male patriarch in leadership and the wife, children, and other household members functioning in their respective roles. What Paul also adds, however, is the strong metaphor of the "headship" of Jesus Christ over all, and he compares the relationship between husband and wife with the relationship between Jesus and the church. A few verses later, husbands are told to "love" their wives, even as they love their "own bodies." This carries echoes of loving one's neighbor as one's own self, the familiar "golden rule." The Greek word for love in both of these instances is *agape,* the fully unselfish, sacrificial love of Christ. In the New Testament there are several Greek words that are translated to the English word "love." Other words imply the love of close friends or sexual expression of love. Paul could have used one of the others in this passage, but throughout he uses the image of Christ giving his life for the church as the basis for the love of husband and wife.

The Marriage Vows Reviewed
For better or worse . . . until we are parted by death.
BCP p. 427

The marriage at Cana is a "reference" to marriage, but there are no vows or words of the actual marriage ceremony that appear in the New Testament. We may assume that early Christians were married using the rite that their culture provided. Jews who had become Christians were married using the Jewish rites. Greeks and Romans used their cultural rites, possibly substituting Christian prayers and blessings for Pagan ones. The traditional marriage vows used by many Christians today appeared in the first English Book of Common Prayer in 1549 and were adapted from earlier English and Latin forms of the liturgy. Taken in context, they refer to one of a series of life experiences—financial, emotional, physical—that make up the continuum of the highs and lows of human life. Within most standard marriage services, there is a clear mandate contained in the vows: mutual regard, support, and respect. Words such as "honor" and "covenant" convey the Christian belief that marriage is meant to strengthen the society in which it occurs. It is not intended as a rite of individuality or isolation, but it is intended by God to give the partners mutual strength so that they may reach out to others—children, parents, those in need.

The marriage vows are one set of many vows that Christians may take over a lifetime in the faith. They are not more or less important than vows that parents take on behalf of their children in baptism or vows taken by those being ordained to ministry. They are taken freely, willingly, and with hope that they provide a framework for continual growth and service. For churches where marriage is considered a sacrament, the vows are taken in the context of

God's blessing and grace, with full knowledge that God's help is necessary. The vows are mutual and equally binding for both parties. They are the signs of a relationship that is covenantal, based on the gift of covenant from God to humanity. They are an ideal to be held and a standard to strive for.

Covenants are the most holy relationships in the Bible. The most important covenants are always between God and humanity. In many cases they were given to one individual on behalf of the community—consider the covenants between God and Noah, Abraham, and Moses. For Christians, the ultimate Covenant is given to all—Jesus Christ—fully human, fully divine. Covenants are more than just agreements or a *quid pro quo* exchange of favors or power. In a covenant, God offers to share a relationship, to share the power of choice, and to entrust the stewardship of creation to the hands of humanity. This is what God did in creation and what is meant in part by being made "in God's image."

In marriage, the husband and wife are joined in a covenant of mutual responsibility and submission of the self for the sake of the other. The new relationship of marriage is a gift, and the man and woman are stewards of the resources of that relationship—social, emotional, economic, and physical. When one partner in a human covenant relationship abuses his or her position, it is equivalent to a steward's abuse of resources held in trust. There is no ownership in marriage, and neither partner is justified in abusing the other, just as we are not justified in abusing the gifts of life and love that God has given us.

When either partner breaks the marriage vows of fidelity and honor, the covenant is damaged. When a partner not only breaks a vow but does nothing to fundamentally change the behavior of abuse, the covenant may be irreparably broken. At that moment, the abuser "makes a critical shift in perspective, no longer seeing [the other] as a human being, equally precious as himself, but only as an object to be manipulated."[8] While the couple has a responsibility to explore alternatives such as counseling and/or temporary separation, these measures should take into account the safety, security, and well-being of the abused and of any innocent bystanders, especially children.

The Holiness of Divorce

The introduction of the Episcopal marriage liturgy includes the words, "therefore marriage is not to be entered into unadvisedly, but reverently, deliberately and in accordance for which it was instituted by God." The same could be said for divorce. Persons who are facing the crumbling of their marriage vows in the face of domestic violence also face the guilt and grief associated with a sense of failure. Even in the best of circumstances, divorce is a very different process than marriage.

When a couple is married, a civil contract and a spiritual covenant is formed. This, however, is not often the focus of the preparation, which instead consists of choosing a wedding dress, planning a reception, arranging a honeymoon, and the other social and cultural rituals. The families are usually supportive, present, and financially generous. Even the churches requiring pre-marital counseling often find couples calling them "late in the game," and couples tend to present their best face to the pastor or minister who counsels them.

In divorce, the situation is reversed. The couple is in crisis, the families are not overjoyed, and the culture offers

---

8. Pamela Cooper-White, *The Cry of Tamar* (Minneapolis, MN: Fortress Press, 1995), 19.

little in the way of support or direction. The civil contract, which seemed so unimportant the day of the wedding, now demands top billing, and the couple must find a way to divide property, recall what belongs to whom, face issues of fairness, and, in some cases, figure out custody of minor children. The couple must face all this complexity in an atmosphere of tension at best and hostility at worst. The guilt associated with a broken spiritual covenant can drive the couple away from the church and harm their spiritual lives.

Couples who separate due to domestic violence often face additional obstacles. In cases where the abuser is incarcerated, the partner outside may not be able to get documents signed or find out where necessary information is located. In cases where the victim is in a secure shelter and may not want the abuser to know the location, cooperation will be more difficult. When a divorce is impending, acquiring legal documents can be a challenge, as can addressing the safety of the abused partner and any minor children.

Christians often feel that the Bible and the church have shut the door on divorce as a godly or acceptable option. This compounds feelings of guilt and shame already present in an abusive situation and may leave victims feeling that they have no spiritual support. In more recent years, however, churches have begun offering alternative views that take domestic violence into account as a justification for divorce.

The Constitution and Canons of the Episcopal Church state: "When marital unity is imperiled by dissension, it shall be the duty, if possible, of either or both parties, before taking legal action, to lay the matter before a Member of the Clergy; it shall be the duty of such Member of the Clergy to act first to protect and promote the physical and emotional safety of those involved and only then, if it be possible, to labor that the parties may be reconciled."[9] This is a clear reference to the possibility that domestic violence may pose a danger for either of the partners and that the responsibility of the minister is to protect the vulnerable.

In essence, this is why divorce exists—to protect the vulnerable. It is a legal option in the United States, fully supported by the United States Constitution, courts, and legislatures. Like many laws that are based on the heritage of jurisprudence inherited from the British Isles, divorce is also based on a Judeo-Christian understanding of what makes a society civilized. Democracy rests on the separation of powers so that the strongest elements of society may not dominate the weaker and more vulnerable.

In many churches, marriage is considered a sacrament, a sign of God's grace in the world. In the best of circumstances, these churches provide or in some cases require pre-marital counseling. Ministers should asses the relationship of the couple for signs of abusive behavior, and educate the couple regarding the qualities of a healthy relationship. They should take all steps necessary to teach and encourage marriage as a mutually responsible commitment.

The role of the church does not stop there. The church should also promote the aspects of healthy marriage and assist couples in their inevitable difficulties. Even when facing abuse, the church may hold marriage as a sacramental grace for couples who are willing to do the hard work necessary to stop the abuse and move toward a safe reconciliation. However, no one should be forced to endure a dangerous or degrading situation for the sake of preserving a marriage, and divorce may be the only solution. Counseling in this

---

9.   The citation is from Title 1, Canon 19, Section 1, p. 57, http://www.episcopalarchives.org/e-archives/canons/CandC_ FINAL _11.29.2006.pdf.

case must be offered in the same holy manner and with the same understanding and compassion with which the church offers assistance to those facing any personal crisis.

In an article in the October 2007 issue of *Christianity Today,* David Instone-Brewer, a senior research fellow in Rabbinics and the New Testament at Tyndale House, Cambridge, presents a new interpretation of Jesus' teaching on divorce. He writes:

> The New Testament presents a problem in under-standing both what the text says about divorce and its pastoral implications. Jesus appears to say that divorce is allowed only if adultery has occurred (Matthew 19:9). . . . Some pastors have found this teaching difficult to accept, because it seems so impractical—even cruel in some situations. It sug-gests that there can be no divorce for physical or emotional abuse, and Paul even seems to forbid separation (1 Corinthians 7:10).[10]

Instone-Brewer re read the texts on divorce after exten-sive research on the rabbinical texts of Jesus' time. A second look from the perspective of a first-century rabbi revealed a new understanding of the Mosaic laws of the time and how they had been applied in first-century Palestine. Jesus rejected a type of divorce for "any cause" that had made it possible for a man to divorce his wife on flimsy charges and take possession of her dowry. In short, Jesus didn't reject the Old Testament, but only a faulty interpretation of it. In addition he didn't reject the "other ground for divorce in the Old Testament, which all Jews accepted . . . [since] every Jew

---

10. http://www.christianitytoday.com/ct/2007/october/20.26. html.

in Jesus' day knew about Exodus 21:10–11, which allowed divorce for neglect. . . . Exodus says that everyone, even a slave wife, had three rights within marriage—the rights to food, clothing, and love." Instone-Bewer relates these three rights to the later development of the Christian marriage vows to love, honor, and keep. In a statement that offers great hope for women in abusive marriages, he writes, "Divorce for neglect included divorce for abuse, because this was extreme neglect. . . . Therefore, while divorce should never happen, God allows it (and subsequent remarriage) when your partner breaks the marriage vows."[11]

---

11. Ibid.

Chapter 3

Providing Support for the Abused

HOW CAN I (GET) HELP?
God alone is my rock and my salvation, my fortress;
I shall never be shaken.

Psalm 62:2

Counselors who assist those in abusive relationships and
law enforcement officers who respond to domestic violence
calls have developed lists of abusive behaviors. In Maryland,
a study sponsored in 2003 by the Maryland Network against
Domestic Violence developed a protocol to provide guidance on what to do when someone is assessed to be in high
danger. Law enforcement officers carry a list composed of
factors that have been found to be present in cases where
domestic violence has resulted in murder or homicide.[1] Law
enforcement officers who respond to a domestic violence
call are encouraged to use the lethality list, and when many
factors are present, encourage the victim to call a local

---

1. http://www.mnadv.org/lethality.html.

hotline. If the victim refuses to call, the officer may use a cell phone to make the call on their behalf.

The following checklist may be used by those who wonder if they are in an abusive relationship, or by a concerned individual who wishes to evaluate the relationship of a family member or friend. Because most abusers are male, the words "his" and "him" are used in the checklist; however, abusers may be male or female.

Signs of Abuse: A Checklist for Adults and Teens

Put a check mark by any that apply to you regarding your husband, wife, boyfriend, girlfriend, partner, or caretaker.

- ☐ Are you frightened by his temper?
- ☐ Are you afraid to disagree with him?
- ☐ Are you constantly apologizing for him, especially when he has treated *you* badly?
- ☐ Does he seem "touchy" and short tempered, display mood swings, yell, swear, or scream when he does not get his way?
- ☐ Does he constantly put you down and then tell you that he loves you?
- ☐ Have you witnessed him beating or abusing a pet, destroying property, or exhibiting reckless or life-threatening behavior?
- ☐ Has he ever thrown things at you, pushed you, kicked you, or shoved you, even "in jest?"
- ☐ Does he tease you in cruel and humiliating ways, call you obscene names, and become offended when you express your feelings of hurt?
- ☐ Does he control all the finances in your relationship and demand an accounting for every penny you spend?

- ☐ Does he try to control what you wear, where you go, and who you are with, expressing jealousy and disapproval that are disproportionate to the situation?
- ☐ Does he spy on you?
- ☐ Does he control your use of the telephone or computer or use technology to monitor your location or behavior?
- ☐ Have you ever left him or separated after living together or being married?
- ☐ Are you pregnant, especially if you know the baby is a boy?
- ☐ Has he ever locked you out of the house or threatened to tell others that you are crazy, unstable, or a terrible person?
- ☐ Is he resentful of your relationships with your family and friends? Does he criticize them and imply that you must choose where your loyalties lie?
- ☐ Do you have a child that he knows is not his?
- ☐ Are you afraid to break up because he has threatened to hurt you or commit suicide if you do leave?
- ☐ Does he tell you that no one else could ever love you or that no one would ever hire you for a job?
- ☐ Has he ever forced you to have sex or engage in sexual behavior you find demeaning?
- ☐ Does he blame alcohol, drugs, or you for his abusive behavior?
- ☐ Has he subjected you to reckless driving, taken away the car keys, or frequently expressed road rage?
- ☐ Are there guns in the house or can he easily get one?
- ☐ Has he threatened to harm your relatives or kidnap your children if you leave?

Add up the number of boxes you checked or each time you said "yes" to a question, and see where your score falls in the section below.

1–10: Your relationship shows signs of tension. You may want to seek counseling or contact one of the hotline listed below. For another evaluation tool, you may want to use the ACTS chart in chapter 4 of this book, which explains Abuse, Characteristic behaviors, Tactics of response and Scriptures of hope, plus descriptions of a healthy relationship.

10–15: Your relationship may be dangerous for you and/or your children. Please seek counseling, or contact one of the hotlines listed below.

More than 15: You are in danger. You do not deserve the violence that is occurring in your life, and you cannot control or change the behavior of your abuser. Your abuser may be breaking the law, and you may want to make a plan to leave and seek the safety of a shelter for abused persons. Call the National Domestic Violence hotline at 1-800-799-SAFE (7233); 1-800-787-3224 (TTY), or consult your local phonebook for resources in your community. You are not alone, and there is help for you.

IDENTIFYING ABUSIVE BEHAVIOR

It is not enemies who taunt me—I could bear that . . .
But it is you, my equal, my companion, my familiar
friend, with whom I kept pleasant company; . . .

Psalm 55:12–14

Since abusers often seem charming, saving their abusive behavior for the private space in their homes, some people might wonder how to recognize abusers or identify characteristics of abusive behavior. The following is a list of abusive behaviors.[2] The more signs a person has, the more likely he or she is to strike out against others in an intimate relationship. In some cases, the abuser may only have two or three behaviors on this list, but they may be in exaggerated form.

Short courtship and quick involvement: Many victims dated or knew their partners for less than six months before they were engaged, married, or living together. The abuser will "come on like a whirlwind" and pressure the other to commit to the relationship, making the other feel guilt for "letting me down" or "hurting me" if the victim wants to slow down or break off involvement.

Unrealistic expectations: Abusive individuals expect their partners to meet all of their needs, to be the perfect spouse, parent, lover, or friend. They state that they expect the other to take care of them and everything in the home, and they often control the relationship through flattery: "I'm all you need—you're all I need."

Jealousy: At the beginning of a relationship, an abuser will say that jealousy is a sign of love. Jealousy is actually a sign of possessiveness and lack of trust. Abusers will question a partner about flirting and time spent with others, particularly family, friends, and children. As time progresses, the abuser may call the partner frequently during the day or stop by unexpectedly at the partner's place of employment. The abuser may refuse to let the partner work and display controlling behaviors such as checking car mileage or asking friends to spy.

---

2. Adapted from the handbook of CASA (Citizens Assisting and Sheltering the Abused) of Washington County, Maryland. Used by permission.

Isolation: The abusive person tries to isolate their partner from all resources, often accusing other people of "causing trouble." The abuser belittles or labels all external relationships as too close and may accuse the victim of sexual infidelity. The abuser may take away forms of communication such as phones, monitor computer use, move the couple to a remote area, or remove transportation alternatives.

Blaming others for problems: If the abuser is unemployed, it is because all employers are "mean" or "unfair." Someone is always "out to get me." The abuser will portray outside authority such as law enforcement as untrustworthy and claim that creditors or business are cheating him or her.

Blames others for feelings: The abuser will blame the partner for upsetting him or her, or for causing anxiety or disorder in the household. Even when the victim tries to change behaviors in response, a no-win situation prevails, and blame continues for a new reason.

The abuser uses feelings, particularly negative feelings, to manipulate the partner. "You make me angry . . . You're hurting me by not doing what I want you to do . . . I can't help myself" are all common refrains. In reality, the abuser chooses feelings and reactions and selectively "loses control."

Hypersensitivity: An abuser is easily insulted and will rant and rave about the injustice of things that are really just part of normal life, such as getting a traffic ticket, being asked to work overtime, or being asked to help with chores. An abuser takes the slightest setbacks as personal attacks and does not like to be criticized or corrected.

Cruelty to animals or children: An abuser punishes animals or children out of proportion to their ability to understand or respond. An abuser is insensitive to their pain or suffering and may expect children to do things beyond their capacity so that the abuser punishes a two-year-old for wetting a diaper. Abusers may bully and tease children or younger brothers or sisters until they cry.

Rigid gender roles: The abuser may expect women to be subservient, saying that the woman must obey in all things, even things that are criminal or go against her wishes. The abuser may see the victim as inferior and responsible for menial tasks, stupid, unable to learn, and dependent.

Sudden mood or behavior changes: Abusers are adept at charming others when they are in social situations outside the home. Sudden changes in behavior confuse many victims who may think their abuser has some kind of mental problem when there is a shift from "normal" to explosive behavior. They may serve in leadership roles in the community or church and be well liked and respected. At home and in private, they may be sullen, moody, tense, and vicious. Following a battering incident of extreme rage or violence, the abuser may turn remorseful, pleading and promising to "do anything" to make up for his bad behavior.

Verbal abuse: In addition to saying things that are meant to be cruel or hurtful, the abuser shows disrespect, curses the partner, and tears down any accomplishments. For example, abusers may call their partners stupid and say that the partner cannot function without them. Verbal abuse may occur at any time and may be timed to wake up a sleeping partner or may follow the return home from a social activity.

"Playful" use of sexual force: The abuser may like to throw down or hold down the partner during sex, act out fantasies

that are degrading, show little concern for the satisfaction or desires of the partner, or force sex when the partner is sleeping or feeling unwell.

Breaking items or striking objects: The abuser may use this behavior as punishment (breaking beloved possessions) or as a threat to terrorize the partner into submission. The abuser may beat on the table, pound the walls, and throw objects near the partner. When questioned, the abuser will declare the right to show frustration in this manner.

Use of force during an argument: The abuser may hold the partner down or physically prevent the partner from leaving the room or the house. Abusers may push or shove their partners or restrain them while forcing them to listen.

RECOGNIZING SIGNS OF ABUSE
. . . my heart is like wax; it is melted within my breast; my mouth is dried up like a potsherd, and my tongue sticks to my jaws; . . .

Psalm 22:14–15

Most victims and abusers are skilled at keeping the silence of domestic violence. There are a few signs, however, that may indicate that someone is a victim of domestic violence. They may not be the signs you suspect, and if you try to confront the victim, they may deny your comments or even become angry with you.

Victims may:

- seem withdrawn, frightened, isolated, unnaturally quiet, reluctant to speak
- overcompensate by being overly involved in programs, perfectionistic, and always cheerful
- appear uncomfortable when with their partner, and may "jump" to serve or please them
- be criticized or belittled by their partner in public, ordered to do things, treated rudely
- make excuses for the partner's bad behavior and minimize outbursts of inappropriate anger
- wear shirts with long sleeves and high necks, or long pants, even in warm weather, to cover new and old bruises, and may wear dark glasses at inappropriate times
- report bad moods and hint at obnoxious events at home
- be insulted in public by her or his children or other family members who will minimize the effect of the remarks, call them "harmless teasing," and dismiss responsibility for them

ACTS CHART OF BEHAVIORS

The following chart of behaviors is adapted from the Power and Control Wheels first developed by the Domestic Abuse Intervention Project in Duluth, Minnesota, with additional material on response tactics from Michelle Pentony, Heartly House, Frederick, MD, 2006. A version of Power and Control Wheels for Native American Women is found on the website of Mending the Sacred Hoop: www.msh-ta.org.

A	C	T	S
Abuse	**Content and Characteristics of Control**	**Tactics and Techniques**	**Scriptures of Hope; Characteristics of Secure and Respectful Relationships**
Coercion and Threats	• Making or carrying out threats to do something to hurt you • Threatening to commit suicide, to report you to the authorities • Pressuring you to drop charges • Pressuring you to do illegal things	• Document each individual threat. If you do not have a secure place to keep documentation, ask a friend or neighbor to keep track of incidents. • Create a safety plan. • Consider legal services. • Identify a safe place to go if you need to leave. • Recognize where you are in the cycle of violence. • Keep your cell phone/911 cell phone with you at all times.	Psalm 140 • Negotiation and fairness • Seeking mutually satisfactory resolutions to conflict • Accepting change • Being willing to compromise

Intimidation	• Making you afraid by using looks, actions, gestures • Smashing or breaking things • Destroying property that belongs to you • Abusing pets • Displaying weapons • Driving recklessly • Abusing children in front of you • Punching walls	• Acknowledge and embrace the things in your life that provide you with a sense of ease and safety. • Believe that you do have control in your life. • Review your safety plan. • Reach out for support and encouragement.	1 Corinthians 13:4–6 • Practicing non-threatening behaviors • Acting so you feel safe, allowing free expression and action
Emotional Abuse	• Using put-downs to make you feel bad about yourself • Calling you names • Playing mind games • Using humiliation • Applying guilt • Suggesting that you are crazy • Insulting your valued beliefs, religion, culture, race, education, heritage, or class • Refusing to socialize with you	• Practice self-care. • Write down things that you are good at. • Remember and revisit things you used to enjoy. • Mobilize your support network. • Engage in counseling services. • Validate your feelings. • Create an emotional safety plan.	James 3:1–18 • Respect • Listening to the other, being emotionally affirming • Valuing opinions • Discussing options

Isolation	• Controlling what you do, read, or watch on TV • Controlling where you go, who you see, limiting your outside involvement, using jealousy to justify actions • Making scenes in front of friends • Checking mileage • Humiliating you in front of others	• Keep a journal with all of your supportive contacts. • Engage in services at your local domestic violence center. • Practice self-care. • Know you are strong and deserve to live a life free of abuse. • Write letters to your friends and family even if you can't send them. • Join a gym, church, PTA, craft group, or engage in team sports.	Isaiah 58:6–12 • Respecting your right to have your own friends, activities, and opinions • Supporting your goals in life • Seeking and allowing outside intervention when needed
Minimizing, Denying, and Blaming	• Making light of the abuse • Not taking the concerns that are raised seriously • Saying the abuse didn't happen • Shifting responsibility for abusive behavior • Saying you caused the abuse	• Know and believe that your thoughts and views are important and matter. • Keep a journal of your thoughts. • Know you don't cause nor deserve the abuse. • Mobilize your support network.	2 Peter 3:14–18 • Accepting responsibility • Admitting wrong • Communicating openly and truthfully

Using Children/ Dependents/ Family	• Making you feel guilty about parenting or caretaking • Using the children to relay messages • Threatening to take children away • Threatening violence against other family members • Using visitations to harass you	• Spend one-on-one time with the children, talking about their feelings. • Learn about the effect of domestic violence on children. • Empower them. • Be a loving and non-violent role model. • Teach them how to call the police in case of an emergency. • Consider counseling for them. • Warn other family members about possible threats and ask them to know their rights and take safety precautions. • Remind them to document any threats they receive.	Psalm 128 • Responsible parenting • Sharing parenting responsibilities • Being a positive and non-violent role model • Respecting in-laws

Dominance	• Treating you like a servant • Making all the big decisions • Acting like the one in charge all the time • Setting strict roles of dominance and submission (male/female; wife/husband; breadwinner/housewife; leader/follower, etc.)	• Know that you have the right to make family and personal decisions. • Work on improving your self-esteem and feeling of self-importance. • Embrace the areas in which you feel strong, stable, and in control. • Examine the dynamics of healthy relationships.	Colossians 3:12–17 • Mutual agreement on household responsibilities • Recognizing and affirming your strengths and abilities • Making major decisions together
Economic Abuse	• Preventing the other from getting or keeping a job • Making the other ask for money • Taking any money the other earns • Denying access to bank accounts or family income • Giving an allowance • Gambling • Filing unnecessary legal charges against you (so you have to take off time from work to go to court or meet with an attorney) • Using money for drugs or alcohol • Refusing to work	• Open your own bank account. • Borrow money from family or friends. • Connect with a job training agency. • Put things in your own name. • Keep records of money you spend and needs that go unmet. • Recognize that what you contribute in time and effort is also part of the economic upkeep of the family.	Matthew 7:7–12 • Making money decisions together • Making sure both partners benefit from financial arrangements • Providing for children • Keeping debt within manageable levels • Sharing account information when needed

Physical Force	• Pushing or shoving you • Slapping, hitting, biting, kicking • Throwing objects at you • Abandoning you in a dangerous place • Refusing to help you when you are sick, injured, or pregnant • Using a weapon against you • Subjecting you to reckless driving • Restraining you	• Keep your cell phone handy. • Call 911 directly after an attack. • Have a backup plan for care if you are ill. • Have a pre-determined place of safety to go to when threatened. • Have cab fare or a friend to call. • Ask any attending physician or medical personnel to document any physical signs of attack.	Luke 1:46–55; 78–79 • Using physical force to compel or intimidate in an intimate relationship is never justified. • If threats are present, outside help is needed.
Sexual threats/ Acts	• Making demeaning remarks about you • Insisting you dress in a more sexual way than you are comfortable with • Criticizing you sexually • Insisting on unwanted touching or advances • Withholding affection • Forcing you to strip when you don't want to • Infidelity • Rape or forcible sex • Sadistic or painful sex	• Realize that sex and love are two different things. • Forcible sex is violence, not love; it is rape and is illegal. • Sex is meant to be a way of bonding and mutual affection. • You have the right to express your feelings of being uncomfortable and to have the respect of your partner.	John 15:12–17 • Love is not forced; it cannot be commanded. • Love is a gift that is given and received with respect. • Sexuality is an expression of that gift and is practiced best in relationships that are committed, long-term, and mutually affirming. • For Christians, sexual intimacy should be expressed within the sacramental bond of marriage.

Spiritual Abuse	• Denying you your ability or right to practice your faith • Insulting your religious beliefs • Insisting that you conform to beliefs that control your access to others • Insisting that you live within a religious community closed to outside interference • Insisting that you must never express doubts or question religious teachings • Insisting that you must obey the direction of religious leaders without question, especially if their directions involve marriage, sex, money, or other areas of personal or family life	• Dangerous cults exercise mind control by using tactics such as sleep deprivation or diets that change body chemistry. Be sure to get enough rest and eat balanced, healthy diets. • Listen to the concerns of others who love you, especially if you have recently joined a church or group. • Read the Bible and other religious books and learn how to interpret scripture for yourself. • Read all holy scriptures in the full context of God's purpose and love for all persons; avoid reading just one verse out of context. • If you feel fearful because of religion, you need to explore the basis of that fear.	Proverbs 12:17 • Healthy religious communities also have ways to allow members to leave. • Religious leaders should be able to explain their positions and allow healthy questions and debate. • Some religions teach the subservience of women. This should not mean that they are to be targets of abuse or that these teachings mean that any person is less than any other. • Peace, love, sharing, and mutual concern are universal religious beliefs.

ASSISTING AN ABUSED PERSON

Is not this the fast that I choose: to loose the bonds
of injustice, to undo the thongs of the yoke, to let the
oppressed go free, and to break every yoke?

Isaiah 58:6

When abuse begins in a relationship, all other relationships
with friends and family change. Rather than becoming
closer, these relationships become strained and distanced.
But, if you love and care for someone whom you know or
suspect is being abused, you can change the relationship
and reach out to establish a mutual connection.[3]

If you suspect that someone you know is being abused,
you should:

- Become familiar with the resources in your community, especially the shelters and domestic violence
hotlines. Provide her the phone numbers and website addresses, and if possible, provide a safe place to
explore these resources.
- Ask: Do you feel safe? Be prepared for defensiveness
and possibly anger when you ask.
- Be discreet; don't put the abused person or yourself
at risk.
- Believe the victim, and let her know that you believe
in her and care for her no matter what. She may see
herself as unworthy of your care.
- Listen and validate the victim's story. Don't tell her
other stories you have heard or your own troubles.

---

3. Susan Brewster, *To be an Anchor In the Storm: A Guide
for Families and friends of Abused Women* (New York: Ballantine
Books, 1997), 20–21.

- Ask if she wants you to help her find a safe place to go if she decides to leave.
- Couples' therapy in abusive situations is often counter-productive, so take care in suggesting where she might go to get help. When in doubt, always refer her to the National Domestic Violence Hotline.
- Offer options, and seek to instill a sense of worth in the victim to uphold her ability to make choices that she feels are right for her.
- Remember that victims often have low self-esteem and may have very little hope left. They may feel exhausted and worn down.
- Tell her that you care for her more than the one who is abusing her.
- Be patient, be consistent, and remain in contact.
- Do not try to confront the abuser. This could put the victim or you in more danger.
- Leaving or correcting an abusive relationship is a long and often arduous process. Be sure that when you offer help, it is within the context of a network of people and resources. This will be best for you and for the person you wish to help.

TO LEAVE OR NOT TO LEAVE

For scoundrels are found among my people; they take over the goods of others. Like fowlers they set a trap; they catch human beings.

Jeremiah 5:26

"Why don't they just leave?" This is a question often asked by those who do not understand the complexities of domestic violence. Many abused women and men are so psychologically and emotionally exhausted, so intimidated and full of shame, that they don't know how to take the first steps back to dignity and self-worth. They have come to believe the words of their abusers—that they are worthless, that no one wants them, that they are stupid and can't do anything right, and that the abuse is their fault.

They may have tried to leave before, but have gone back when their partners promised to stop the abuse. They may not know about the "remorse" phase of the cycle of abuse when the abuser tends to back off and beg to be forgiven, before escalating the tensions again. They may be afraid for their lives or the lives of their children. They may have been deprived of learning any job skills and may not have any way to support themselves and their children. They may have come from abusive families and have no support system or examples of healthy relationships. Their abusers may tell them that they cannot leave or the abusers will commit suicide, or kill or harm them, a particularly powerful threat when there are firearms present in the household. They may be convinced that God wants them to stay to preserve the marriage or that their abuser is the only one who really loves them. They may believe it is their mission to redeem, change, or save the abuser. They may feel they have failed to figure out how to adapt or change in order to stop the abuse.

Many abused people are in a constant state of stress. This does not put them in a good position to make major, life-changing decisions. Prolonged stress and fear can give victims symptoms of traumatic stress disorder, which may take months or years to resolve.

BARRIERS TO SEEKING HELP
Out of the depths I cry to you, O Lord.

Psalm 130:1

The good news is that, in general, battered persons do not passively endure physical abuse but actively seek assistance from various sources. Some studies show that by the time abuse victims leave a relationship for good, they have contacted five or more sources of help prior to entering a shelter. They may have visited a doctor or confided family stress to a friend. They may have sought counseling from a minister without specifically reporting abuse. They may have sent some "signals" of distress to those who know how to read them. The following list shows some of the barriers to leaving an abusive relationship[4]:

Fear: A battered person who has received physical abuse or who lives in a home where firearms are present may face physical danger when attempting to leave. Leaving the home does not guarantee that the abuse will end, as the abuser may continue to search for the victim and punish the person for leaving. Battered people understand the limited ability of the criminal justice system to offer long-term protection, especially when there are threats but no actual incidents to report.

Love/emotional ties: Many abused people love their partners. They want the violence, not the relationship, to end. They hold on in the hope that the battering will stop. They have difficulty accepting the fact that they cannot influence

---

4. Adapted from the handbook of CASA (Citizens Assisting and Sheltering the Abused) of Washington County, Maryland. Used by permission.

the abuser to change his or her behavior. They feel responsible for providing stability and are often locked into the dependency of the abuser.

Economic dependency: When a woman leaves the home, there is a 50% chance that her standard of living will drop below the poverty level. In some cases the abuser has taken control of the family finances. Those who choose to leave face a daunting process of applying for aid and assistance, recreating tax forms and other family records, and overcoming the shame they feel in asking for help.

Denial: The cycle of violence centers on the reinforcement of denial. Particularly in the first instance of abuse, the victim may believe it is a one-time exception. It may be a long time before another battering incident occurs, and the victim may not recognize the cycle of violence.

Shame and guilt: Family, ministers, friends, and cultural morays may communicate that the fault lies in the victims, that the victims need to be better wives, better husbands, or better parents. If victims were abused as children, they grew up with a sense of shame and low self-esteem. They may believe they are the cause of the abuse and deserve the treatment they receive.

Belief that the children need a father/mother: Some parents endure physical and emotional abuse in order to keep the family intact for the sake of the children. When violence overflows onto the children, the parent may take that as a signal to leave the relationship. Unfortunately, in about half of the households where domestic violence is taking place, it is also directed at the children.

Isolation: The abuser imposes isolation on the partner, putting an end to contacts with family and friends who might find out about the abuse. The victim may comply with this isolation out of shame and a sense of duty to protect the partner's reputation and job. Isolation also cuts the victim off from contacts that may help correct false and dysfunctional thinking and beliefs about the cause of the abuse.

Fear of government: In immigrant families, victims may believe that they could be deported or jailed if they seek legal help. Abusers will use this fear for intimidation, and may threaten to report their partners to local officials. In any family the abuser may threaten to report the other parent as an unfit mother or father and have the children taken away.

Societal conditioning: Learned society, cultural, and religious beliefs may contribute to the sense of duty to keep the marriage together at all costs.

Lack of support: In smaller communities, victims face issues of finding a safe place to go or other resources. They may not have access or transportation to sources of assistance.

Learned helplessness: After repeated beatings and constant threats, the victim may be convinced that it is useless to try to leave. The victim psychologically shuts down and withdraws.

JUST FOR MEN: MEN WHO ARE ABUSED
Surely many houses shall be desolate, large and
beautiful houses, without inhabitant.

Isaiah 5:9

Men are also victims of domestic violence. While they may
be caught up in the same cycles of violence, their experiences are different from those of women in significant
ways. While women report that fear is their most familiar
emotion, men who are abused experience humiliation and
shame. For them abuse often takes the form of emotional
and psychological control and manipulation. Their partners may abuse them verbally, accuse them of not providing
enough money or attention, and make threats over custody
of children. They may feel guilty and powerless. If the relationship ends, they may continue to receive threats and
worry that their reputation may be unfairly damaged.

Men in genuinely abusive relationships are much less
likely to seek help. They may not realize that many local
domestic violence programs also offer services to men
who are abused. They may feel very isolated and unable
to cope. Most of the literature about abuse is written for
women, as they are the victims most of the time; men may
not be able to apply the ideas and concepts to their lives
and experience.

The church may respond to men who are expressing
painful relationships by providing a listening ear and appropriate resources for referral. Men who are abused need to be
believed and encouraged to seek ways to respond and set
boundaries on the manipulation of their intimate partners.

Be skeptical, however, when men assert that males are
abused at the same rate or with the same severity as females.
Many studies show that women are 7 to 10 times more likely

to be injured in acts of intimate violence and are financially and socially more locked into marriage than men. Blaming the victim is not a helpful approach towards bringing peace and safety to our homes.[5] Weigh reports of women hitting their male partners against a backdrop of self-defense against a larger and stronger adversary.

FOR PEOPLE IN SAME-SEX RELATIONSHIPS
I am utterly spent and crushed; I groan because of the tumult of my heart.

Psalm 38:8

While many of the aforementioned abuses also occur in same-sex relationships, some factors are magnified. Isolation is a prevalent condition for those whose families may not know they are gay and who may also wish to be discreet about their relationships. Abusers may threaten to "out" a partner or otherwise expose intimate details to a victim's boss, family, or church. The secrecy that surrounds many same-sex relationships is compounded by negative societal factors and used as a force of intimidation by an abuser. In most states even long-standing same-sex relationships are not recognized by the legal system, and there is complicated legal recourse to arrange protective orders, custody of children, or distribution of property in case of separation.

---

5. Kate Orman, quoted in Michael Flood, "Claims about Husband Battering," http://www.xyonline.net/husbandbattering/shtml.

ADVICE FOR CHURCH LEADERS

Be careful then how you live, not as unwise people
but as wise.

Ephesians 5:15

Ministers who have not learned about the cycle of violence
or about the characteristics of abusers can do great harm to
a victim of abuse who approaches them about counseling.
The church, so supportive of marriage, does not seem to
offer the same support for those seeking a place safe from
abuse. In the worst cases, well-meaning ministers have
urged women to try harder, to return to the relationship,
and by their humility to seek to change the heart of the
abuser. When approached by a person seeking help or asking questions about a difficult relationship, ministers need
to be aware of their own prejudices and preferences, both
scriptural and theological. Do you blame the victim for
weakness and the inability to stand up and set boundaries?
Do you feel the victim may be contributing to the tension
or making the abuser mad? Do you work so hard to protect
the sanctity of the marriage that you forget about the safety
of the individuals and their long-term well being?

These are some practical steps that ministers can take to
help the abused:

- The Episcopal Church General Convention Resolution
  1988-D064 urges each diocese to "establish and
  conduct training workshops for ministers and laity
  to identify the signs of battering. . . ." Attend such
  a workshop if it is offered, or invite your diocesan
  trainers to hold one in your area.
- Network with other churches in your community to
  increase your awareness of support systems for victims of domestic violence.

- Contact the local professionals for domestic violence assistance in your area or community. Get to know them. They are your best resource.
- Address the issue of domestic violence in pre-marital counseling. Be specific and upfront. If necessary, use the checklist in this book in a one-on-one session with a prospective bride.
- Address the issue of abuse when you are asked to perform couples counseling. Be aware of the pitfalls of counseling couples, and be prepared to refer them to someone with specialized training and experience. Be very aware of the degree of denial that exists in violent relationships. If possible, interview the man and woman separately.
- When you preach on the covenant of marriage and the family, include the sin of abuse.
- Remember that the Episcopal Church General Convention of 2000 revised the Marriage Canon to state that "When marital unity is imperiled by dissension, it shall be the duty . . . of such Member of the Clergy to act first to protect and promote the physical and emotional safety of those involved and only then, if it be possible, to labor that the parties may be reconciled." [Title 1, Canon 19, Section 1]
- Do not be drawn in and triangulated by the abusers. They will come seeking justification and using words such as "forgiveness" and "reconciliation" in order to keep control in an abusive relationship.
- Become familiar with your local law-enforcement professionals. Know the facts on *ex parte* or protection orders—what they are, what they include, how to obtain them.

- Keep confidentiality. However, if you suspect that a person may be in danger of bodily harm, you must act as necessary to protect life. Have a plan ahead of time!

WHEN IT IS TIME TO LEAVE

I will both lie down and sleep in peace; for you alone,
O Lord, make me lie down in safety.

Psalm 4:8

If you or someone you know has expressed a wish to leave the abusive situation, be prepared with the following advice. Remember that the most lethal period in an abusive relationship is the time when separation is occuring or just after leaving. Do everything with "safety first" in mind—your own safety and the safety of the person you are trying to help.[6]

Help the victim make a plan:
- Where will she go? Are there family or friends with whom she can stay? Where is the nearest domestic violence shelter?
- Does she want to call the police to obtain a protective order? Will she testify against her abuser?

Prepare an escape kit that contains most or all of the following items:
- Photo ID such as driver's license, passport, student ID, green card

---

6. "It Shouldn't Hurt to Go Home," Maryland Network Against Domestic Violence booklet, adapted from the original booklet created by the Idaho Coalition Against Sexual and Domestic Violence (revised September 2003).

- Social security card
- Cell phone and charger
- Cash and/or a bank card, check book or record of all bank accounts, if possible a credit card in her name, welfare cards, social security number(s)[7]
- Insurance and medical cards for herself and her children
- A change of clothes, jacket, toothbrush, personal items; same for any children
- An extra set of keys to the house and the car
- At least two days' supply of prescription medicines
- A list of emergency phone numbers
- Birth certificates, bank books, important papers

Rehearse her departure:
- Under what conditions may it be "safe" to leave?
- Where will she go first?
- What resources are immediately available for her to keep her safe?
- Under what conditions might she agree to return home to retrieve personal items?
- Is she ready to make a "clean break"?
- Is she ready to seek a separation, divorce, and/or protection of the law?

If she is not planning to leave or vacillates, help the victim consider two major questions:
- What is the worst thing that could happen if I stay?
- What is the worst thing that could happen if I leave?

---

7. Consider opening a separate bank account in your name only. Abusers may close accounts after a victim leaves.

Help her consider some coping strategies:

- What will be the factor that will help her make a decision to call the police?
- If she is unable to call for protection, is there a signal she can arrange with neighbors or friends? Has she taught the children to call 911? Is 911 programmed into her cell phone?
- What kind of strategies has she worked out to minimize the threat of physical harm? Have they been effective?
- Can she anticipate the escalation of violence and get out of the way in time?
- Does she have a support network? Are there family members, friends, or a faith community whom she believes cares for her and can help?
- Does she know the phone number or website of the nearest domestic violence program or shelter?
- Are there weapons in the home? Can they be removed or placed in a safe, locked area, separate from ammunition?

After she has left the relationship, help her consider how she will[8]:

- Change the locks if she is still in the home and the abuser has left.
- Install security features such as lights, motion detectors, gates, smoke detectors, metal doors.

---

8. Laws concerning legal separation and protections offered by the courts differ from state to state. Some of the following actions must be backed up by legal documents, restraining orders, custody agreements, or other civil actions. Victims should obtain advice from the legal counsel at a local domestic violence facility, or the district courts. Some of the necessary information about the types of protective orders that are available is online on the government websites.

- Inform her neighbors that her former partner is not welcome. Ask them to contact law enforcement officials if they see that person around the property or in the area.
- Make sure that those who care for her children—day care, school, private teachers—know who does and who does not have permission to pick up the children.
- Obtain a civil order for separation and keep it near her at all times.
- Let her boss and co-workers know about her situation, and ask for security at her workplace.
- Get counseling, attend workshops, and join support groups; form a supportive network that can help her sort out her feelings and help her make good decisions about her future.

IS THERE HOPE FOR AN ABUSER?
Rescue us from the evil one.

Matthew 6:13

A review of the literature regarding the characteristics of abusive personalities is complex and inconclusive. As Christians, we are called to hold out hope even in hopeless situations. We are called to forgive and work for reconciliation. We are called to love with mutual respect. At the same time, abuse is an act of evil, and those who abuse others are morally responsible for their behavior. Although we might seek to understand them, we cannot excuse their behavior and must seek to protect those who are victims.

What causes someone to abuse and act in violent ways toward an intimate partner, spouse, parent, or child? Is it nurture or nature? Can the tendency toward violent behavior be mitigated or channeled into more positive outcomes? Can abusers learn not to abuse? Is it possible to change? We have already reviewed in this text the cycle of violence and the danger of the period of "remorse." Are abusers really sorry for their behavior? In many cases they certainly seem to be, but what they do with their sorrow and remorse in the long run is the deciding factor.

Many experts contend that violence is a learned behavior—the result of nurturing— especially if the abuser was abused as a child or teen. They believe that such learned behavior has a chance of being changed if the abuser is willing to undergo extensive intervention and counseling from a professional trained in domestic violence issues. Abusers may be frightened, insecure persons, fearful of abandonment. They typically have tremendous feelings of jealousy. Their violence may be a learned response that was demonstrated in their family of origin. They may have grown up in an environment where women were not respected, where power was the ruling force, and where "manliness" was equated with control over others. When a man with this sort of background is paired with a woman who was also abused and grew up in a situation where her boundaries were not secure or respected, the situation is ripe for an outbreak of abuse.

The Christian faith has a great deal to say about how members of a family treat one another. Someone who has been nurtured in violence may be able to look around and see alternatives in marriages and families that function without violent outbursts. Children of these families may be nurtured and taught as they participate in Christian formation and youth activities. The cycle of violence can be broken from one generation to another if proper intervention is made, and the parties involved are intentional about the long and hard work necessary for reform and reconciliation.

New studies are showing, however, that controlling and violent behavior may also be the result of nature, that a person may not have a fully developed conscience and, therefore, has no true remorse or empathy. Dr. Martha Stout, a clinical psychologist, contends that about 4% of the American population are true sociopaths—by her definition, persons who do not have a conscience. They may intellectually understand the difference between right and wrong, but they suffer no remorse from their actions and feel no responsibility for the harm they do to others. These men and women are not usually criminals and are often charming and, in the eyes of the world, powerful and successful. However, they use fear and intimidation to accomplish their goal of always winning, always "being right," measured by their own set of standards.

According to Stout, most of us cannot identify or recognize these individuals as being anything out of the ordinary. One aspect, however, seems to be prevalent in their make-up. The tip-off is the pity play. When confronted by their controlling and manipulative behavior, they are able to gain the sympathy of others. Pity is an emotion we usually reserve for those who have been unjustly victimized and for the innocent or the vulnerable.[9]

Abusers who have this disorder are experts at keeping the cycle of violence spinning. Any time those they control appear to be seeking a way out, they seize upon any vulnerable point, show copious remorse, moan about their loss of control, promise to change their behavior, and even enter counseling or receive some other form of intervention, just as long as the cycle is not broken and their intimate partner stays in the relationship. Even if the

9.   Martha Stout, *The Sociopath Next Door* (New York: Broadway Books, 2005), 107.

relationship ends in divorce, this type of abuser will seek out another vulnerable person and recount the terrible experience with the previous partner, thus eliciting new emotions of pity and sympathy.

This type of manipulative behavior may also be found in cases where the woman is the abuser and the man is the abused. Women who manipulate and control others, playing on their sympathy and at the same time tearing down the self-image of their partner, are just as abusive as men who do the same. This type of abuse is more hidden and harder to identify. When men examine their relationships and identify with the methods of control and manipulation listed in this text, they may want to seek counseling and help.

Whatever the cause of the abusive behavior, the most important response is to stop the abuse and seek safety for the victim. There is no justification for domestic violence, and no amount of analysis or reasoning is needed for intervention and assistance. In fact, many victims may spend a great deal of time trying to understand their abusive partners, trying to "fix" what is wrong, looking for excuses, and, as a result, delay the necessary response and intervention to stop the cycle and even save their lives.

Chapter 4

Breaking the Cycle

STRATEGIES FOR PREVENTION

"I will show you what someone is like who comes
to me, hears my words, and acts on them. That one
is like a man building a house, who dug deeply and
laid the foundation on rock; when a flood arose, the
river burst against that house but could not shake it,
because it had been well built."

Luke 6:47–48

There is an old saying that you can only spend so much time
pulling drowning people from a river without eventually
going upstream to find out who is throwing them in. Denial
and silence push victims into the flood of domestic violence. The church is wonderfully and uniquely equipped to
provide prevention strategies that may keep young women
and men safe and teach them how to choose and nurture
healthy relationships.

The church is one of the only communities left in the
United States where people from all generations gather in
one place and share their lives. Ours is a culture of separation

and individuality, of competition and power, where intimate relationships, especially the marriage bond, are expected to handle all the stress and inevitable problems of life. Men and women enter a relationship believing in love, avoiding loneliness, and seeking support. They believe that this relationship will provide for their personal emotional needs and that in marriage they will find someone who will understand them and make them happy. Marriage is expected to be a ticket to fulfillment, security, and life-long satisfaction.

The church knows that good marriages do not exist in a vacuum. One of my seminary professors once said that if a couple does not "eat the bread" of Jesus Christ, they will end up cannibalizing each other. The multigenerational community of the church provides a wonderful laboratory in which young people can receive guidance, learn to identify and choose healthy relationships, and ask for help from others who care for them. Faith in God reminds us that we are not alone and that there is a greater purpose to our existence than we can often see or perceive. The church is also a place to bring the pain of our lives where we might find it accepted, understood, and eventually healed.

DYNAMICS OF HEALTHY RELATIONSHIPS[1]

The good person out of the good treasure of the heart produces good, and the evil person out of evil treasure produces evil.

Luke 6:45

Building a good relationship takes time and displays mutuality. Take time to learn about yourself and to recognize the signs of a healthy relationship:

1. www.wvdhhr.org/bph/trust/index.htm.

Look inward: Who are you? What do you want to be? Do you love and respect yourself or has your experience of life up to now been one of abusive relationships?

Look outward: What are the qualities you most admire in others? What is most important to you in a relationship?

Include family and friends: Healthy relationships are not isolating or exclusive. Healthy couples enjoy getting to know one another's family and friends and feel good about introducing the partner to them.

Support one another: Trust is important in healthy relationships. The couple can discuss priorities, have fun with each other, relax, and feel safe. Each feels the other person wants what is best for them, according to what each has expressed.

Make your feelings clear: Don't just go along to keep the peace. Express yourself when you feel uncomfortable or threatened. Tell the other person when your feelings are hurt and why. Trust and respect your own feelings enough to make sure the other person listens to you.

Promote respect: In healthy relationships, the individuals make decisions about things together. Neither person gets his or her own way all the time. Don't put the other person down in front of others. Foster a sense of humor that is genuine and playful.

HELPING BOYS BECOME MEN[2]

You then, my child, be strong in the grace that is in Christ Jesus.

2 Timothy 2:1

Boys need advice on how to behave toward girls. They receive mixed messages about power, domination, control, and manhood as they watch TV, play video games and sports, and observe the behaviors of men around them. They need to know that violence does not equal strength and that gentleness and respect do not imply weakness. Steps can be taken to provide boys with good role models and options for their relationships. Men can take positive action toward ending domestic violence by teaching and showing the boys they know about treating others with respect and honoring their decisions.

Be there for the boys in your life. Spend time with them. Listen to them. Demonstrate respectful reactions in frustrating situations such as slow traffic or waiting in a restaurant. Teach polite replies to those in authority or in service positions. Demonstrate strategies for handling tense or potentially violent situations. Find out about the role models boys admire the most, and discuss why their role models may or may not respect women. Fathers may be the greatest influence in this area of a boy's life. He will notice if his father's attitude toward his mother changes between public and private settings. He will learn subtle attitudes displayed by his father toward women in general, including women in positions of authority and women who are sexually attractive.

---

2. http://toolkit.endabuse.org/GetToWork/Workwithyoung-men/HowBoys.html.

If you are a young man reading this, ask yourself: Are there boys I know who make jokes about girls and put them down? What words do I use or hear that degrade women or make them into objects? How can I learn to respect myself and others? Seek out a man you trust—your father, coach, teacher, minister—and ask him about how to relate to women.

Practice the "golden rule" when you are dating. How would you want to be treated? Treat the girl with the same respect. Before taking a girl out on a date, take time to meet her parents, and spend time getting to know her friends. Group dates can be a great way to compare and contrast how girls and boys act towards each other. Ask your girlfriend what makes her happy, what her dreams and ambitions are, and share your hopes and dreams with her. Play "by the rules," and end your dates on time and in a manner that both of you find comfortable.

While it is natural to be curious, spending time looking at pictures of women on websites or in magazines tends to make them into objects of desire. Instead, spend time getting to know the real people in your life. If your girlfriend ends the relationship, you may feel rejected and hurt, but respect her right to say no. Respect yourself enough to know that new relationships are possible. Being hurt is not an excuse for hurting others, and there is never an excuse for hitting someone in an intimate relationship. If you have trouble controlling your impulses and are afraid that you might hurt the one you love, seek professional help. It is never too late to learn to respect yourself and others.

JUST FOR MEN:
WHAT MEN CAN DO TO END
MEN'S VIOLENCE AGAINST WOMEN
Be subject to one another out of reverence for Christ.
Ephesians 5:21

In the last few decades, great strides have been made toward getting men involved in responding to domestic violence. This is an essential move that churches can support by providing information for men and encouraging them to examine their attitudes toward women and the sexism in our culture. The social norms that define "manhood" need to be shifted away from a power-based system, and men must challenge the behavior of their peers when it displays denigration of women. One group that is leading the way in this effort is "A Call to Men" (www.acalltomen.com). Their website states that "ending violence against women is primarily the responsibility of men . . . well-meaning men . . . men who for the most part don't see themselves as part of the problem . . . need to get involved." Every time a man does nothing to challenge the behavior of abusive peers, he is a part of the silence that surrounds the issue of domestic violence. By characterizing the problem of domestic violence as chiefly a "women's issue," men collude with socially defined roles that tolerate violence against women and blame the victim.

When men work with women to create systems of accountability, men who are abusive are singled out and cannot look to their male counterparts to support them or overlook their behavior. Men can also challenge the notion that abuse is due to mental illness, poor anger-management skills, chemical dependency, stress, or any factor other than the bad behavior of the abuser and a system of socialization that continues the historic oppression of women. Men in the church have a special responsibility to reinterpret the scriptures that seem to give men permission to hold control over others and assume an inordinate amount of power in marriage or other intimate situations. We must hold men who claim to love their partners yet abuse them accountable to the standards of scripture that condemn such behavior.

TEACHING GIRLS TO SAY "NO"
There is no fear in love, but perfect love casts out fear.
1 John 4:18

Churches are full of young women who are learning the virtues of the Gospel of love and forgiveness. What we also need to teach them are the signs of genuine love and the hard journey of true forgiveness. Girls in our culture are taught to be polite and say "yes" even when they may feel like saying "no." They need to recognize that in certain circumstances "no" is also a word of grace, an acceptable answer, a response that deserves respect. They need to be taught about good boundaries, to learn that their intuition is trustworthy, and that men who try too hard to prove they are well-intentioned are sometimes the most dangerous of all.

Young women learn about dating from movies and TV shows. A common Hollywood formula is: Boy wants Girl, Girl doesn't want Boy, Boy persists and harasses Girl, Boy gets Girl.[3] Girls are taught to be nice, even when rejecting unwanted advances. Many young men are taught that when she says "no," she is playing "hard to get" and that she doesn't really mean it. Girls learn that they must play "hard to get" when that is not what they really mean. Young women are

3.   Gavin de Becker, "Teaching Teenage Girls to Say No," http://life.familyeducation.com/teen/safety/36353.html.

not taught how to get out of unwanted relationships, and young Christian women are taught that rejecting someone is "not being nice." Boys who cannot let go choose girls who cannot say no, and a dangerous dynamic is created. The complexity of teen-age relationships, fueled by the natural processes of young maturation and the desire to break away from family and religious authority, leaves young women in a vulnerable position.

The church must teach young women that persuasion is not a passive but a positive internal choice. Men and boys who are insecure or who are acting from abusive relationships will seek to control others through physical power, intimidation, and emotional manipulation. While it is almost impossible to prevent young women from being targets of unwanted attention from boys and men, they do not have to become victims.

Young women can learn about the cycle of violence and be forewarned about short, intense courtships that seem "too good to be true." We can teach them to recognize relationships of unequal power, and techniques of emotional bullying and manipulation. They can learn to exercise caution when the person approaching them urges them to be private or seeks to control the environment to shut out family, friends, or regular social activities.

If you are a young woman reading this chapter, and you are just beginning to date, review the dynamics of healthy relationships. There are ways you can learn to get rid of unwanted attention. The cardinal rule is this: *Do not negotiate.* Once you have made a decision that you don't want a relationship with a particular person, once you tell him that you do not want to date him or talk to him, the other person should respect your position. Almost any contact after that rejection may be interpreted as negotiation. If you continue to get unwanted attention, ignore it for a while, and then respond after the tenth try, the pursuer learns that you will eventually give in. Response will be seen as progress. Trying to explain your position will not help someone who cannot hear the word "no." Remember, if a boy continues to pursue, he is, in effect, saying that he does not accept your decision. End any relationship with someone who does not recognize or respect your feelings.

If you are a young woman reading this chapter and you think you may be in an abusive relationship, review the characteristics of abusers found on pages 7–12 of this book. If your boyfriend displays controlling behavior, if he is seeking to isolate or dominate you, or if he has ever hit or threatened you with physical harm, please seek help. Learn to recognize the cycle of violence, particularly the cool-down or honeymoon phases. If your boyfriend makes you feel guilty, puts you down, forces you to do things you are not comfortable doing, uses drugs or alcohol and pressures you to use them, takes or controls your money, is possessive or jealous, or hurts you but then shows great remorse and promises to treat you right, these are danger signs. Review the signs of healthy relationships at the beginning of this chapter.

If you have ended a relationship, and your former boyfriend asks you to forgive him and take him back, exercise extreme caution. Be suspicious of remorse that sounds desperate and shows no sign of changed behavior. True forgiveness is a gift, not a right or something that another can demand of you. Forgiveness takes time and is a journey of respect for your own feelings and choices.

Chapter 5

Church Advocacy

Give justice to the weak and the orphan; maintain the right of the lowly and the destitute. Rescue the weak and the needy; deliver them from the hand of the wicked.

Psalm 82:3–4

In the article "Facing an Unwelcome Truth," Janice Shaw Crouse writes:

> We must face an unwelcome truth: Many of the attacks on the church come from women who have experienced great pain in their lives, either because someone in the church caused their pain or they found the church impotent in response. . . . As Christians, we are meant to be burden-bearers. We are meant to have a heart for the hopeless, for the

weary, for the abused. And yet, the church needs to do better in this area.[1]

Since the early 1980s, churches have responded to the issue of domestic violence, providing materials for education and awareness. Since I am an Episcopal priest, I am most familiar with the resolutions and actions of my own church. In addition, the Episcopal Church shares a close relationship with the Lutheran and United Methodist churches, both in history and practice. The following section reviews the approach of these three churches to the issue of domestic violence:

The Episcopal Church

Episcopal Church policy on the issue of domestic violence has been addressed by the representatives to the tri-annual General Conventions—meetings consisting of lay delegates, clergy delegates, and bishops from the entire Episcopal Church. The church is divided into geographic areas called dioceses. Each diocese has at least one bishop and multiple congregations. The dioceses elect representatives who attend the Conventions and decide on the direction of the church's mission and ministry.

In 1985, the Episcopal Church passed a resolution with a commitment to ". . . raising the awareness of Episcopalians about violence and measures to oppose violence; to examining the effects of violence within ourselves and our institutions; and to sharing strategies which enable Christian people to support and develop programs that confront the issues of violence and open the way for actively opposing

---

1. http://www.christianitytoday.com/ct/2005/october/21.87.html.

violent behavior." The resolution instructed each diocese to "provide and promote programs at each internal level that will raise Episcopalians' consciousness of violence in their lives and in the institutions of church and society, at the same time equipping them with understandings and strategies of actively opposing violence that will permit them to change attitudes and behavior grounded in the many forms of violence: poverty, racism, human and national relationships, drug dependency, ecological insults, ageism, crime, *domestic brutality* and other forms of destructive behavior."[2]

In 1988, the General Convention passed a resolution specifically designed to direct each Diocese to: (1) establish and conduct training workshops for clergy and laity to identify the signs of battering and sexual abuse of women and children; (2) produce a register for the clergy and laity of available resources within their communities, such as support services, shelters, and entitlement programs; and (3) encourage clergy and laity to consult with and refer victims to professionally trained counselors and support groups. The resolution concluded by urging "the seminaries of the church to include in their curricula appropriate education and training in the area of family violence."[3]

In 1991, the problem of domestic violence was named specifically in a resolution about Violence in Society: "*Resolved*, the House of Bishops concurring, That the 70th General Convention call upon the Church at every level to renew a commitment to address violence in every sector of

2. Resolution 1985–D021, *Journal of the General Convention of . . . The Episcopal Church, Anaheim, 1985* (New York: General Convention, 1986), 243, http://www.episcopalchurch.org. Italics mine.

3. Resolution 1988–D064,*Journal of the General Convention of . . . The Episcopal Church, Detroit, 1988* (New York: General Convention, 1989), 277, http://www.episcopalchurch.org.

society, especially that of domestic violence aimed toward spouses, children and older adults;" and "That parishes and dioceses be urged to develop educational programs and resources through preaching, through liturgy, through pastoral care for both the victims and the perpetrators of all kinds of violence and through advocacy with the public sector for programs of education, social service and public policy that will address the problems of violence."[4]

At the General Convention in 2000, two more resolutions were passed providing specific suggestions for follow-up and action: One encouraged "every congregation within the church to designate at least one Sunday each year during one of the following months: a. April (National Sexual Abuse Prevention and Sexual Assault Awareness Month) or b. May (Child Abuse and Neglect Prevention Month) or c. October (National Domestic Violence Awareness Month) for special prayers for all whose lives have been affected by any form of sexual, domestic, or family violence, remembering in particular those who have been violated by sexual misconduct within the Church." An additional provision called upon "the National Church Center to make available to every congregation within the church educational opportunities for its members about practical, pastoral, spiritual, and/or theological issues related to the problems of sexual or domestic violence and call upon congregations to make an active and ongoing response to these problems in their local community."[5]

---

4. Resolution 1991-C022, *Journal of the General Convention of . . . The Episcopal Church, Phoenix, 1991* (New York: General Convention, 1992), 388, http://www.episcopalchurch.org.

5. Resolution 2000-C025, *Journal of the General Convention of . . . The Episcopal Church, Denver, 2000* (New York: General Convention, 2001), 326–27, http://www.episcopalchurch.org.

A second resolution that year called upon "state governments to promote and enact statutes addressing the reduction of Domestic Violence and the protection of victims of Domestic Violence and child neglect."[6]

The Episcopal Church consistently acknowledged and worked to address domestic violence and the need to teach and practice peacemaking as a spiritual and moral duty. Accordingly, at the General Convention in 2000, a "Pledge of Nonviolence" was approved and commended to the whole church:

> *Resolved*, That each congregation of the Episcopal Church become a model for peacemaking in our violent society by encouraging its members to commit themselves to nonviolent and peaceable behavior in their relationships with others at home, at school, at work, at church, in the community, and wherever they find themselves; and be it further *Resolved*, That every congregation also encourage its members to adopt The Pledge of Nonviolence as it comes from the Institute for Peace and Justice, St. Louis, Missouri:

> Making peace must start within ourselves. I commit myself to become, with God's help, a nonviolent and peaceable person.

> To respect myself, to affirm others and to avoid uncaring criticism, hateful words, physical attacks and self-destructive behavior.

---

6. Resolution 2000–D073, *Journal of the General Convention of . . . The Episcopal Church, Denver, 2000* (New York: General Convention, 2000), 680, http://www.episcopalchurch.org.

To share my feelings honestly, to look for safe ways to express my anger and to work at solving problems peacefully.

To listen carefully to one another, especially those who disagree with me, and to consider others' feelings and needs rather than insisting on having my own way.

To apologize and make amends when I have hurt another, to forgive others and to keep from holding grudges.

To treat the environment and all living things, including our pets, with respect and care.

To select entertainment and toys that support healthy values and to avoid entertainment that makes violence look exciting, funny or acceptable.

To challenge violence in all its forms whenever I encounter it, whether at home, at school, at work, at church or in the community and to stand with others who are treated unfairly.

This is my pledge. These are my goals. I will check myself on what I have pledged once a month for the next twelve months so that I can help myself and others become more peaceable people.[7]

---

7.   Resolution 2000-A058, *Journal of the General Convention of . . . The Episcopal Church, Denver, 2000* (New York: General Convention, 2000), 212, http://www.episcopalchurch.org.

The Evangelical Lutheran Church in America

The Lutheran Church (ELCA) has also provided legislative and educational resources related to the issue of domestic violence. A recent check of their national website (www. elca.org) reveals a message approved by the board of the Division for Church and Society and adopted by the ELCA Council on April 18, 1994. It calls on church members to "consider how they might become more involved in countering the reality and fear of violence in their communities." The statement notes that although violence seems timeless, there are disturbingly new aspects of brutality shown in news reports, hate crimes, and violence in the home. The causes of this violence are outlined as complex, citing poverty, economic injustice, the breakdown of community institutions, inadequate moral formation, and substance abuse, among other factors. The people of the church are challenged and encouraged to be peacemakers and to minister to those in captivity to violence by providing safe places, mediating, educating, assisting, supporting organizational efforts, building relationships, and enabling people to reclaim their communities. While this statement was not written just about domestic violence, it addresses the general issues that contribute to the atmosphere in which such violence is ignored, justified, or condoned. Multiple worship and Biblical resources are listed on the website under "The Decade for a Culture of Peace and Nonviolence."

An article published in 2004 called "Nurture Families Dealing with Domestic Violence" by Marta Poling-Goldenne[8] provides a helpful list of what individuals and congregations

---

8.   http://archive.elca.org/christianeducation/lifetransitions/ pdf/domesticviolence.pdf. Copyright 2004 Evangelical Lutheran Church in America.

can do to assist families struggling with domestic violence. Many of the principles listed are incorporated in this book. The article further states that domestic violence affects ". . . women inside and outside the pews of congregations." In an article in the October 2004 issue of *Lutheran Woman Today*,[9] Havilah L. Tower-Perkins, a media relations coordinator for the National Domestic Violence Hotline and the Texas Council on Family Violence wrote: "Domestic violence is one of the few issues that affects us all." She tells the story about a young woman who called a shelter from a busy mall while her husband was running in and out of stores searching for her. The woman was safely picked up and received care at a nearby shelter. The article lists hotline numbers and encourages the readers to remain open-minded and not blame the victims by questioning their behavior.

The United Methodist Church

The United Methodist Church website[10] states, "The General Board of Church and Society of The United Methodist Church names domestic violence as a priority issue of the church confession" and "that our denomination has been too silent about this 'pandemic', happening not only in the United States, but around the world." The statement continues, "Tragically, Christian women often feel compelled to stay in abusive relationships by Scripture telling them to 'submit to their husbands,' or 'turn the other cheek.' Abused women often feel abandoned by God."

---

9.   www.lutheranwomantoday.org/back/04issues/1004article3.html.

10.   www.umc-gbcs.org

An article in the UMC Book of Resolutions reads, "The church is challenged to listen to the stories of victims and survivors and to seek information and guidance that will lead to wiser and more effective ways of ministry with persons who experience domestic violence and sexual abuse. The church must be a refuge for people who are hurting, and it is an entirely appropriate place for these issues to be addressed."[11]

The 2004 Social Principles contain a section on "The Nurturing Community" that outlines the church's approach and beliefs about the family, marriage, divorce, and other related issues. Section "H" is titled "Family Violence and Abuse": "We recognize that family violence and abuse in all its forms—verbal, psychological, physical, sexual—is detrimental to the covenant of the human community. We encourage the church to provide a safe environment, counsel, and support for the victim. While we deplore the actions of the abuser, we affirm that person to be in need of God's redeeming love."[12]

The General Board of Church and Society advertizes a one-day seminar on domestic violence for local churches and/or conferences, including a variety of worship materials and resources for action and education. The United Methodist Church is a member of several legislative groups and coalitions that actively seek protection for women and children in abusive situations.

---

11. "Violence Against Women and Children," 2004 Book of Resolutions, 186, found on UMC website, http://www.umc-gbcs. org/site/ apps/nlnet/content.aspx?c=frLJK2PKLqF&b= 3784561&content_id={9A1D24A2-4885-4C71-9DEFC6E7ED3065D5} &notoc=1.

12. The Nurturing Community, http://www.umc-gbcs.org/ site/c.frLJK2PKLqF/b.3713149/k.E2F3/182161_The_Nurturing_ Community/apps/nl/newsletter.asp

An article on the church website by Jim Winkler[13] promotes October as Domestic Violence Awareness Month and urges churches to take at least one action to address violence in their communities, and to take a fresh look at the scriptures and theological messages that seem to validate violence against women. In an accompanying article, Linda Bales also urges churches to speak out against domestic violence, citing a personal story of finding a friend, her face bruised after her step-father broke her mother's jaw and then turned on her. Linda states that she was shocked to find that the mother was a member of her church. She wondered if her pastor had ever offered respite for those experiencing domestic violence.[14]

If you are wondering what your particular church is doing about domestic violence, start with your minister or another leader at your church. If you do not find resources handy at your place of worship, take action, using the list of suggestions in the next chapter. If you have a home computer on line, go to the home page of your denomination's website and enter "domestic violence" on the search line, if there is one, or call the contact number listed on the "contact us" page. You can also go to your local library and use the computer there to search for resources.

Today most churches have attempted to address the issue of domestic violence through education, advocacy, and legislation. The Southern Baptist Convention website, for example, contains a resolution that condemns domestic violence.[15]

---

13.   http://www.umc-gbcs.org/site/apps/nlnet/content3.aspx?c=frLJK2PKLqF&b=2901991&ct=4207861.

14.   http://www.umc.org/site/apps/nlnet/content3.aspx?c=lwL4KnN1LtH&b=2072519&ct=4545489.

15.   http://www.sbc.net/resolutions/amResolutionasp?ID=1078.

The website of the Assemblies of God USA has an extensive section on domestic abuse, including an article by Grant L. Martin on "What Pastors Can Do to Help Victims of Domestic Violence in the Church."[16]

A search of the website of the United States Conference of Catholic Bishops resulted in a large number of articles and accompanying suggestions for laity and clergy facing domestic violence issues.[17]

A statement issued by the USCCB, November 12, 2002, strongly condemns Domestic Violence, saying, "The Catholic Church teaches that violence against another person in any form fails to treat that person as someone worthy of love. Instead, it treats the person as an object to be used. When violence occurs within a sacramental marriage, the abused spouse may question, 'How do these violent acts relate to my promise to take my spouse for better or for worse?' The person being assaulted needs to know that acting to end the abuse does not violate the marriage promises." A downloadable powerpoint presentation to educate laity and clergy is also available from this website.[18]

WHAT YOUR CHURCH CAN DO

For I am convinced that neither death, nor life, nor angels, nor rulers, nor things present, nor things to come, nor powers, nor height, nor depth, nor anything else in all creation, will be able to separate us from the love of god in Christ Jesus our Lord.

Romans 8:38–39

---

16. http://enrichmentjournal.ag.org/200704/200704_122_Dom-Violence.cfm.

17. http://www.usccb.org/laity/women/violence.shtml.

18. http://www.usccb.org/laity/help.shtml.

Awareness and Education

Always assume that there are people in your pews who have experienced or are experiencing abuse. Be aware of the subtle messages that the church sends through programs, sermons, and activities that promote the assumption that "everyone here is okay and every marriage and relationship is healthy."

Make an intentional plan to educate church members and leaders and raise awareness of the issues involved in domestic violence. The church council, vestry, or advisory board may make a commitment to nonviolence and to the promotion of healthy communication in the church and in their homes. Communicate that decision and reach into every group and program of your church—from worship to Christian formation, from outreach to pastoral care. Use the resources in this book and from other sources as guidelines to a comprehensive and cross-generational approach to making your church a "safe house" for those whose lives are affected by domestic violence.

Designate one Sunday a year during April (National Sexual Abuse Prevention and Sexual Assault Awareness month) or October (National Domestic Violence Awareness month) for special prayers and educational opportunities. Remember to include something that reaches your teens and kids, too! If you have a parish nurse, she or he will be able to help you. Enlist the assistance of members who are lawyers, counselors, teachers, law enforcement officers, or any other public servants in planning activities and worship. Domestic Violence Awareness Month (DVAM) began in 1995 and is now hosted by the Domestic Violence Awareness Project. More information about this organization and ideas for DVAM may be found in the list of resources in the back of this book.

Provide written materials about domestic violence on your tract racks, bulletin boards, or any public place. Just as important, put literature in a few private places as well. Make sure there is a display rack on the *back* of the door in the women's restroom that is kept filled with a variety of current literature about domestic violence.

Provide the local hotline number and a key website and/ or email address for domestic violence programs on small business-size cards (blank cards which can be used in a printer or copier are for sale at any local office supply store) that women can put in a pocket or wallet. Place the cards in strategic areas around your church building such as the bathrooms, the kitchen, the nursery, and on bulletin boards.

Provide a copy of this book or other related literature in your tract rack, lobby, waiting area, or anywhere else people congregate. There is a great deal of free material available, so whether your church is small or large, you can provide what is helpful. There is also plenty of material that may be copied from online websites. Consult the resource list in the back of this book.

Invite counselors from a local shelter to speak on a Sunday morning to your adults and youth. Encourage any church committees and groups, especially your youth group, to host a speaker on domestic violence.

Include an article about domestic violence in your bulletin or newsletter with the phone numbers and websites of hotlines and resources. Some examples are included beginning on page 109.

Set up a box for donation of unwanted wireless phones along with their chargers and batteries. Donated phones are either recycled or re-used through a partnership with providers who will activate phones to be used for 911 calls only. (Be sure to tell donors to erase any memory on the phone prior to donation.)

Work with your youth to sponsor Valentine's Day information cards that educate about domestic violence and promote appropriate behavior. Valentine's Day materials, including sample letters for publicity, poster, cards, commitment petitions, and bookmarks, are available from the National Resource Center on Domestic Violence.[19]

Ideas for Preaching, Worship, and Bible Study

- Observe Domestic Violence Sunday during October, using the materials provided through your national church organization or diocese, or the free resources listed in the bibliography of this book.
- Hold a Bible study on some of the "Texts of Terror" that reveal experiences of abuse suffered by our biblical ancestors.
- Provide prayers in the liturgy from time to time that lift up victims of abuse and call for justice for their abusers.
- In cooperation with a local shelter or domestic violence program, host a special worship service for those recovering from abuse.

Advocacy

- Become informed about legislation designed to help victims of domestic violence. Vote to support laws that protect the rights of the abused.
- Support local law enforcement officials. Ask them to speak to your groups about how they handle domestic violence, legal rights for victims, and the proper way to report suspected abuse and rape.
- Contact your local shelter and obtain a list of items they need. Print the list in your bulletin or newsletter,

19. http://new.vawnet.org/Assoc_Files_VAWnet/NRC_valentine02.pdf.

and ask for donations for the shelter or program to assist battered persons and their families. (This will have a dual purpose of helping your local program and making its programs familiar to your members!)

- Share information about domestic violence with the professional and business people in your church. Ask them to see what is being done in their workplace to help victims and provide services. Here are some specific suggestions for those in various professions:

  — *Physicians*: Medical coalitions against domestic violence provide ideas for assessment, documentation, and diagnosis of physical abuse. According to Colleen Moore, coordinator of the Family Violence Response Program at Mercy Hospital Center in Baltimore, 50% of the victims of domestic violence are treated at one time or another by a physician while only 4% actively seek help from a domestic violence shelter. Symptoms of domestic violence may manifest in depression, fatigue, headaches, ulcers, and other stress-related ailments, and those who seek treatment for external bruises may also be victims of hidden strangulation, only seen if the attending physical or medical personnel are trained and sensitized to look for the tell-tale signs.[20] Physicians may shy away from involvement in cases of suspected domestic violence out of concern for the time they think it will take to deal with the situation. The Maryland Medical Society has a chart that demonstrates that the time to asses a victim of domestic violence is no longer

20. Panel discussion, "The Effects of Abuse on Individuals and the Community," Hood College, Frederick, Md. (April 3, 2008).

than the time needed to asses a person with *angina pectoris* (chest pain due to heart disease).

— *Business owners/managers/employers*: The workplace may feel like a safe place for victims of abuse, but if not properly prepared, it may also be a place of danger. According to national statistics, homicide is the second leading cause of death on the job for women. Corporations are taking steps to begin peer programs for CEOs to help them create an atmosphere of safety through the use of posters, publications, articles in company magazines, and safety plans for enforcing protective orders. Companies can provide encouragement for women to report abuse, stalking, and interference with their jobs, one of the tactics used by abusers to isolate their victims and cause them to lose their jobs. AllState Insurance Company has an extensive section on domestic violence on their website, providing an example for other businesses and corporations.[21]

— *Educators*: Ask your school or institution to include education about the cycle of violence in appropriate curriculum. Report any abusive behavior you witness or suspect. Promote respectful behavior in the classroom and on the campus. Talk to your school's counselor about providing free resources for students and teachers to take home, and about involving students in outreach and advocacy to prepare students for healthy social interactions. Involve male teachers,

---

21. http://www.allstate.com/foundation/econ-empowerment. aspx.

especially coaches and other athletic instructors, in talking to boys about abusive behaviors. Use materials from organizations such as "A Call to Men,"[22] which specializes in speaking to athletes about the abuse of male power and privilege.

— *In your neighborhood*: If you suspect that domestic violence is taking place, report suspicious behavior to the appropriate law enforcement authority. Document any incident you witness, and if the victim obtains a protective order, offer to share your information with legal counsel. Support community events that provide safety skills, help you get to know your neighbors, and work cooperatively with support services. If you live in an apartment with a public bulletin board, post the name and number of the local shelter and provide free literature in appropriate locations.

Sample Articles for Church Bulletin or Newsletter:

She may be sitting next to you or across the room. She may seem perfectly normal. He may be a member of your vestry, church council, or board or be a trusted leader in your community. Each of them may be experiencing the darkness of domestic violence. Each of them or you may be a victim, or an abuser. The fact is 1 out of every 3 women will be the victim of domestic violence in her lifetime. The Center for Disease Control and Prevention estimates that over 1 million incidents of violence occur against a current or former spouse, boyfriend, or

---

22. http://www.acalltomen.org

girlfriend per year.[23] Don't say, "It doesn't happen here!" Indifference is not an option when it comes to domestic violence. If you or someone you know has been abused, seek help today. Remember, our Baptismal Covenant calls us to "respect the dignity of every human being," including ourselves! [List local contacts or use the list provided in Resources section of this book]

It shouldn't hurt to go home, but for 4 million American women each year, home may be the place of assault and abuse. Domestic violence is one of the "hidden" sins of our society. No one ever asks to be hit, and no one deserves to live in fear and intimidation. Domestic violence is a pattern of coercive behavior characterized by the domination and control of one person over another. It can take the form of emotional, psychological, economic, and verbal abuse, not just physical abuse. If you think you or someone you know may be in an abusive relationship, seek help from [list local hotline]. Don't wait until you or your loved one becomes a statistic. Don't wait to reclaim the abundant life God has planned for you.

"But I love him/her!" Does your boyfriend or girlfriend try to make you feel guilty for wanting to spend time with other friends? Does he or she want to know where you are all the time? Does he or she control your money, insist on telling you what to wear, bully, or threaten you? Perhaps he or she has hurt you, shoved you, forced sex on you, pushed you,

---

23. http://www.ncadv.org/files/domesticviolencefacts.pdf.

or humiliated you in front of your friends. Then he or she apologizes and promises not to do it again . . . only it happens again, and each time it gets a little worse. These are warning signs of an emotionally abusive relationship. If someone hurts you, forces you to do something you do not want to do, or makes you feel scared or bad in any way, it is important to talk about it with a trusted adult. You can also go online at [list website] or call [list local hotline]. It isn't your fault, and you cannot change the other person. It won't get any better, and you will never find just the right behavior to make it go away. But you can decide to embrace the hope that God loves you more than any human can. God's love *never* hurts.

Worship in Your Local Church

Each church has its own pattern of worship. It is often best to begin with the familiar liturgy and add special prayers for domestic violence, or to ask your minister to preach on this issue. Many churches have liturgies covering the issue of domestic violence, which are ready to use. There are many opportunities within worship to draw the attention of church members to the sin of domestic violence and to gather the resources of the community of faith. Other complete services may be found at the website www.sabbathofdomsticpeace.org. The Mennonite Church furnishes prayers for victims of domestic violence on their website, www.mcc.org, and the Evangelical Covenant Church provides a collection of resources including a Call to Worship, scripture texts, litanies, prayers, and responsive readings on it's website.[24]

---

24. http://www.covchurch.org/cov/resources/women-ministries/worship-resources-for-domestic-violence-awareness.

Prayers within your liturgy
(These petitions may be added to the Prayers of the People
in the Episcopal Book of Common Prayer):

Form I: For victims of domestic violence and for all who advocate for them, let us pray to the Lord.

Lord, have mercy.

Form II: I ask your prayers for those who live in homes where there is violence and abuse. Pray for those in danger that they may be relieved and protected.

Silence

Form III: We pray for all whose homes are torn by domestic violence.

Bring them to a place of safety and peace.

Form IV: Uphold all who are afraid to go home, whose lives are torn by strife and domestic violence; give us the wisdom and courage to support and assist them.

Silence

Lord, in your mercy

Hear our prayer.

Form V: For those whose homes are places of danger and violence; for those who live in fear, intimidated by those they love; and for all who offer counsel, help, and assistance to them.

Lord, have mercy.

Form VI: For all whose lives are torn by domestic violence; *For all who minister and care for them.*

Collect.

Gracious God, like a mother hen you shelter us under your wings: Bring your truth and love into homes where domestic violence has shattered the peace. Provide sustenance for the victims and accountability for the abusers. Send wise and courageous friends who can offer alternatives, and bring your healing power into broken relationships. May your church provide a haven of safety and peace for the abused and reach out to support all who serve the needs of the abused in our communities; through Jesus Christ, our Lord. *Amen.*

SPECIAL WORSHIP SERVICES FOR SURVIVORS OF DOMESTIC VIOLENCE

To you, O Lord, I lift up my soul. O my God, in you I trust; do not let me be put to shame; do not let my enemies exult over me.

Psalm 25:1–2

During October, your local domestic violence program may want to hold a service of remembrance and support for the victims of domestic violence. When planning a community service, the following guidelines may be helpful:

- Determine whether the service will be Christian or multi-faith.

- Gather ideas and solicit cooperation from various religious leaders—both clergy and laity. Determine whether the service will involve community leaders and elected officials, or if it is primarily for those whose lives have been affected by domestic violence. Plan accordingly.
- Determine a venue that is safe, accessible, inviting, and easily located.
- Be prepared for persons who may be uncomfortable or who may be suddenly overwhelmed by emotions. Provide a safe, quiet room for any who might want to leave quickly. Have ushers available to point out the bathrooms, or persons trained as supporters who can quickly and quietly stand by with a comforting word, patience to hear anger and grief, and resources for referral.
- Some participants may be uncomfortable with closeness or touch. It may not be a good idea to request that the participants hold hands while praying. If anointing and/or prayers for healing are offered, some may not want to participate.
- An order of service should be provided, which should include contact numbers for local shelters or domestic violence services.
- Avoid proselytizing or promotional materials that sound like the event is an invitation to join a church.
- When choosing music, read the words carefully to be sure that the selections you make do not support dominance or use militaristic or gender-specific phrases.

Suggested Order of Service (assuming a Christian setting)

Gathering:

Instrumental music may be played before the service.

A leader may give welcome, offer an explanation for the service, and provide directions.

Provide a glass bowl or other attractive container, slips of paper, and pencils. Participants may write the names or initials of those they know who have been victims of domestic violence. During the procession the bowl is placed on the altar or a central table.

A gathering song may be sung. Selections will vary according to your tradition. The following is a list of possible hymns that may be used throughout the service:

Amazing Grace
Just as I am
God will Take Care of You
Morning has Broken
Jesu, Jesu, Fill Us With Your Love
Precious Lord, Take My Hand
We Shall Overcome
There is a Balm in Gilead
Savior, like a Shepherd Lead Us
What a Friend We Have in Jesus
Love Divine, All Loves Excelling
It's Me, O Lord, Standing in the Need of Prayer
Just a Closer Walk with Thee

Gathering words:

Leader: Blessed be the One, Holy and Living God.
Assembly: *God is our hope, present in times of trouble.*
Leader: Let us pray:
(Silence is kept)
God, who from chaos and darkness created the world and all that is in it; we come before you with the broken pieces of lives lived in fear, asking for your healing and your peace. Come among us to make a new creation in our lives as we gather in support and unity; grant us your hope and help us to see your light. We pray in your holy name. *Amen.*

Reading(s) from Scripture:

Any number may be used. They may be read by a variety of persons. At the end of each reading, the reader may say: "Hear what the Spirit is saying to the people." The people respond: "thanks be to God."

Mathew 5:1–12
Psalm 118:5–14
Psalm 139:1–12
Psalm 89:1–4, 24–29
Psalm 91:16
Psalm 18:1–616–33
Psalm 31:1–24
Psalm 61:1–5
Psalm 62:1–12
Proverbs 24:11–12
Luke 2:46–55
John 8:2–11
John 7:37–38
Mark: 5:24b–34
1 Corinthians 13:1–7
Romans 8:22–27, 31–39

Music may be played between the readings

Commentary on Readings:
   This may take the form of a short sermon (10–15 minutes), discussion of the passages, storytelling, silence, journaling, drawing, finger-painting, or other expressive art.

At this time the leader may introduce all those present who have given their permission to be identified as resource persons, representatives of agencies who assist the abused, law enforcement, clergy, and counselors. The assembly may be invited to meet them after the service at a reception with light refreshments. Refreshments offered should be healthful and attractive. Additional tables in the hospitality area may be set up for displays of brochures or other information.

An additional hymn or song may be sung here.

Prayers:
   (These or others may be used.)

Dear God, our Creator, we gather today because we care about those affected by domestic violence: women, children, and men.
   We remember those who have lost their lives to this malfunction in our society. We pray that their souls are now at rest.
   We remember children living in homes of domestic violence. Deliver and protect them from further harm.
   We pray for perpetrators, that they may seek help. Help them to relinquish their need to exert power and control.
   We remember current victims whose lives are filled with fear and uncertainty, those who are trapped in the psychological cycle of violence and abuse, hope and false love. We

ask that you give them a new vision. Guide them with your wisdom to make sound choices that will lead to new life.

We pray that religious leaders will end scriptural abuse so that they may no longer contribute to the oppression of women.

We give thanks for those who dedicate their lives to providing education, shelter, and support.

Finally, O gracious God, be present with us, restore peace and hope that we may persevere with your Holy Spirit. In faith we pray, *Amen.*[25]

Litany:

Leader: God of Justice, open our eyes to the reality of domestic violence and give us courage and compassion to respond to victims and survivors.

Assembly: *Out of the depths we call to you, O God. Hear our voice.*

Leader: Christ, you became a servant to all. Break down the pedestals of power and privilege that exalt human power over the power of your love, and help us see ourselves and others as created in your image.

Assembly: *Out of the depths we call to you, O God. Hear our voice.*

Leader: Holy Spirit, you breathe through our prayers and give life to the world. We offer our anger and resentments, our fear and pain, our broken hopes and fearful hearts. Pour out your healing balm and allow us to let go of the darkness in our lives.

---

25. The Rev. Angela Shepherd, *Women's Uncommon Prayers*, edited by Elizabeth Rankin Geitz, Marjorie A. Burke and Ann Smith, Council of Women's Ministries/Domestic and Foreign Missionary Society of the Protestant Episcopal Church, USA (Harrisburg: Morehouse Publishing, 2000), 73.

Assembly: *Out of the depths we call to you, O God. Hear our voice.*

Leader: We pray for those who in arrogance need to control the lives of others. Help them to see the error of their ways and turn their hearts.

Assembly: *Out of the depths we call to you, O God. Hear our voice.*

Leader: We pray that women and men may find ways to affirm the respect they deserve and the support they need without taking it from others.

Assembly: *Out of the depths we call to you, O God. Hear our voice.*

Leader: We admit that we have lost control at times and poured verbal coals of anger and frustration on others. Forgive us and help us to let go of these past hurts.

Assembly: *Out of the depths we call to you, O God. Hear our voice.*

Leader: Help us, in the midst of conflict, to find ways of responding that bring life and true reconciliation, while protecting the dignity of everyone.

Assembly: *Out of the depths we call to you, O God. Hear our voice.*

Leader: Help all communities of faith to offer a place of refuge and understanding and avoid using scriptural abuse to confuse and oppress the vulnerable.

Assembly: *Out of the depths we call to you, O God. Hear our voice.*

Leader: Help us all to build and support systems in our community that hold abusers accountable and provide for the care and comfort of victims of domestic violence.

Assembly: *Out of the depths we call to you, O God. Hear our voice.*

Additional prayers may be written or found in various publications. One excellent resource is *The Bridge to Forgiveness: Stories and Prayers for Finding God and Restoring Wholeness*, by Karyn D. Kedar, published by Jewish Lights Publishing, Woodstock, VT, 2007.

Exchange of the Peace:

Leader: May the Peace of God be with this assembly!

Assembly: *May we know the Peace of God.*

Those present may greet each other with a sign of "peace."

If they have not been made before, introductions of resource persons and announcements may be made at this time.

Blessing and Dismissal:

Leader: May the God of Peace lead us into all peace.

Assembly: *Amen.*

Leader: May Christ, the God among us, keep us from harm this night/day.

Assembly: *Amen.*

Leader: May the Holy Spirit lead us towards the truth that sets captives free.

Assembly: *Amen.*

Leader: May God the Holy Trinity bless us this night/day and always.

Assembly: *Amen.*

Resources

ORGANIZATIONS

The National Domestic Violence HotlineAdvocates are available 24 hours a day, 7 days a week for victims and anyone calling on their behalf to provide crisis intervention, safety planning, information and referrals to agencies in all 50 states, Puerto Rico and the U.S. Virgin Islands. Assistance is available in English and Spanish with access to more than 170 languages through interpreter services.

www.ndvh.org; 1-800-799-SAFE (7233);
TTY 1-800-787-3224

www.seeitandstopit.org

Created for teens and young adults to educate about the dangers of abusive behaviors. Provides online activities and ways to be an advocate against abuse.

FaithTrust Institute

Provides religious leaders and community advocates with the tools and knowledge they need to address the religious and cultural issues related to abuse.

2400 North 45th Street, Suite 110, Seattle, WA 98103, 1-877-860-2255, 202-634-0055. Fax 206-634-0115; e-mail: info@ faithtrustinstitute.org; website: www.faithtrustinstitute.org

Violence Against Women Network (VAWnet)

An online resource for advocates working to end domestic violence, sexual assault, and other violence in the lives of women and their children.

6400 Flank Drive, Suite 1300,
Harrisburg, PA. 17112-2778;
Voice 1-800-537-2238, TTY 1-800-553-2508;
Fax 717-545-9456;
www.vawnet.org

Mending the Sacred Hoop

Resources for Native American women.
www.mch.ta.org

www.endabuse.org

Provides materials on "Coaching Boys into Men."

Office on Violence Against Women, United States Department of Justice

Provides federal leadership to reduce violence against women, and to administer justice for and strengthen services to all victims of domestic violence, dating violence, sexual assault, and stalking. Includes contact information for organizations that provide help with these issues.

www.ovw.usdoj.gov

National Coalition Against Domestic Violence

A thirty-year-old coalition of local, state, regional, and national organizations helping to provide safe alternatives, such as shelters, program, public education, policy development, and legislation on matters pertaining to domestic violence concerns. The site contains extensive resources.

www.ncadv.org

PASCH, Peace and Safety in the Christian Home
Sponsors a national conference and publishes excellent newsletters reflecting on scripture and abuse.
www.peaceandsafety.com

Domestic Violence Awareness Project
Partnership of local, tribal, state, and national domestic violence organizations and networks.
www.nrcdv.org

National Network to End Domestic Violence
A social change organization dedicated to creating a social, political and economic environment in which violence against women no longer exists.
www.nnedv.org

A Call to Men
A group committed to ending violence against women by addressing and educating men and boys.
www.acalltomen.com

The Center on Violence and Recovery
This center promotes two intimate abuse interventions: a criminal justice–based model called "Peacemaking Circles," and a pre-arrest, community-based model, called "Healing Circles." Both interventions draw on restorative justice principles and emphasize healing offenders, victims, and their families, to stop the transmission of violence from one generation to the next.
http://www.nyu.edu/cvr/intimate/ivr_programs.html

BOOKS

Cooper-White, Pamela, *The Cry of Tamar: Violence Against Women and the Church's Response.* Minneapolis, Minn.: Fortress Press, 1995.

Fortune, Marie M., ed., *Violence against Women and Children: A Christian Theological Sourcebook.* New York: Continuum, 1995.

Kroeger, Catherine Clark and Nancy Nason-Clark, *No Place for Abuse: Biblical and Practical Resources to Counteract Domestic Violence.* Downers Grove, Ill.: Intervarsity Press, 2001.

Stout, Martha, *The Sociopath Next Door.* New York: Broadway Books, 2005.

Trible, Phyllis, *Texts of Terror: Literary-Feminist Readings of Biblical Narratives.* Philadelphia: Fortress Press, 1984.

DVD AND VHS

(available for purchase at http://www.faithtrustinstitute.org/)

Webpage for ordering: http://www.faithtrustinstitute.org/index.php?p=Domestic_Violence&s=33

Pastoral Care for Domestic Violence: Case Studies for Clergy Now Available for Jewish and Christian Audiences

Broken Vows: Religious Perspectives on Domestic Violence (also available in Spanish: *Promesas Quebrantadas*)

Wings Like a Dove: Healing for the Abused Christian Woman

Domestic Violence: What Churches Can Do